THE AUTOHARP

Complete Method And Music
(With 150 Selections)

Compiled And Arranged by
ALEXANDER SHEALY

Illustrated by Marga Anto

FOREWORD

The AUTOHARP was invented by Charles Zimmerman, patented in 1883 and first produced in Philadelphia, in 1885.

It is used principally to accompany group and solo singing, but it has become increasingly popular in recent years in rhythm bands, orchestras and solo performances. It is a versatile instrument, comparatively easy to learn, and very popular in camps, schools, hospitals and churches all over the world.

The songs in this book were selected because they are familiar to most people and lend themselves to the harmonies produced on the instrument. We have included songs in just about every popular category:

Juvenile songs, great for beginners
Ballads, old and new, for entertainment and special occasions
Folk songs featured by leading folk singers
Holiday songs, especially for the Christmas season
Familiar hymns, spirituals and patriotic songs
Songs of to-day

The chords are shown at points that emphasize basic rhythms. All of the songs can be played on the 12 and 15 bar Autoharps, and a large number of selections can be played on the 5 bar instruments.

May you derive much pleasure from the use of this effective instrument.

THE PUBLISHER

CONTENTS

ELEMENTARY MUSIC PRINCIPLES

You don't have to read music to play the AUTOHARP, but certain elementary principles may be helpful. For example:

Music is divided into TIME UNITS (measures) pictured on a STAFF (5 lines and 4 spaces) on which music notes are placed.

The illustration to the right is a STAFF. It opens with a CLEF sign.
The vertical lines divide the staff into measures to impart regularity
  to the music.
Notes go through the lines or in the spaces. Some notes are below or
  above the limited compass of the Staff. Such notes are expressed
  by short lines added below or above the Staff, called "leger lines".

These are MUSIC NOTES | Notes on the Lines | Notes in the Spaces | Leger Notes

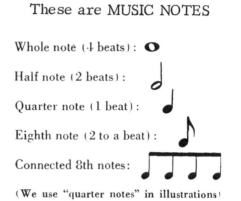

Whole note (4 beats) : **O**

Half note (2 beats) :

Quarter note (1 beat) :

Eighth note (2 to a beat) :

Connected 8th notes :

(We use "quarter notes" in illustrations)

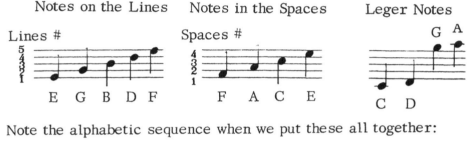

Note the alphabetic sequence when we put these all together:

The white and black notes on your AUTOHARP follow each other by HALF-TONE intervals. The illustrations above are WHOLE TONES which can be lowered or raised to the next half-tone by means of FLATS (♭) to lower a tone and SHARPS (♯) to raise a tone.   A sign like this (♮) is called a NATURAL, which restores a flatted or sharped note to its basic tone.

The presence of one or more FLATS or SHARPS after the CLEF SIGN means that every note in the piece is flatted or sharped. For instance, a flat on the middle line (B) means that every B becomes B♭, a sharp on the top line (F) means that every F becomes F♯.

Before each piece of music, you will see a "TIME SIGNATURE", like $\frac{2}{4}$ $\frac{3}{4}$ $\frac{4}{4}$ or C (same as $\frac{4}{4}$).

$\frac{2}{4}$ time means 2 beats to a measure, a popular tempo for polkas and one-steps. $\frac{3}{4}$ time means 3 beats to a measure, used mainly for waltzes. $\frac{4}{4}$ or C time means 4 beats to a measure, used in most dance music, popular songs and ballads.

A dot after a note increases its value 50%. For instance, a dotted HALF NOTE 𝅗𝅥• takes 3 beats.

Each note has its equivalent in SILENT value, like this: (called "rests")

WHOLE REST | HALF NOTE REST | QUARTER NOTE REST | 1/8TH REST

Some notes are tied with marks like this ♩‿♩ which means to hold the first note for the full time value of both notes.

CORRESPONDING LETTERS PRINTED ON YOUR AUTOHARP KEYBOARD WILL ASSIST YOU IN ASSOCIATING THE MUSIC NOTES ABOVE ILLUSTRATED WITH THE NOTES ON THE AUTOHARP.

PRELIMINARY NOTES

The AUTOHARP comes in various sizes. The smallest size has 5 bars across the strings. On this instrument you can play 5 chords:

$$B\flat \qquad C \qquad C7 \qquad F \qquad G7$$

The 12-bar Autoharp adds the following chords: (Note small "m" means "minor chord")

$$A7 \qquad Am \qquad D7 \qquad Dm \qquad E7 \qquad G \qquad Gm$$

In the key of F - identified in your music with a flat ($\flat$) sign following a clef ($\clubsuit$) sign, you will usually find F, B$\flat$ and C7 chords.

In the key of C - identified in your music with a clef ($\clubsuit$) alone, you will usually find C, F and G7 chords.

THE KEY OF F   THE KEY OF C

The music in this book is confined to the chords named above..... many of the pieces in this book require the simple basic chords found on the smallest of the instruments.

Look at the chord listings at the head of each piece. If the chords are B$\flat$, C, C7, F and G7, you can play the selections on the smallest of the Autoharps.

The 15-bar Autoharps add additional chords, for instance, chords in the key of D.

The diagram below shows the chord arrangements on the 15-bar Autoharp; all chords to the right of the diagonal line are the 12-bar chords. The 5-bar chords are starred (*).

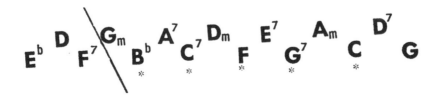

TUNING

The Autoharp will stay in tune for many months if handled with care.

DO NOT PLACE IT NEAR RADIATORS, DIRECT SUNLIGHT or OPEN WINDOWS.

Locate middle C and, with your tuning key, tune middle C to middle C of a piano, pitch-pipe or tuning fork.

Tune by octaves. (An octave, in the language of music, is the interval between the 1st and 8th notes of a scale, like from C to C - so it encompasses the same tone, lower or higher.) Tune the C's, then down the other octaves, the F's, the G's, and the tones with flats and sharps till the strings correspond in pitch to the tuning instrument.

Turn the key to the LEFT to LOWER the tone, to the RIGHT to RAISE the tone. Pluck the string as you turn the tuning key.

IMPORTANT! Turn the key gently to avoid breaking string. A very small turn does the trick.

When all strings correspond (at least approximately) in pitch to the tuning instrument, test the chords. Press each bar and stroke the strings. Then adjust the "off strings" until each chord is in perfect balance.

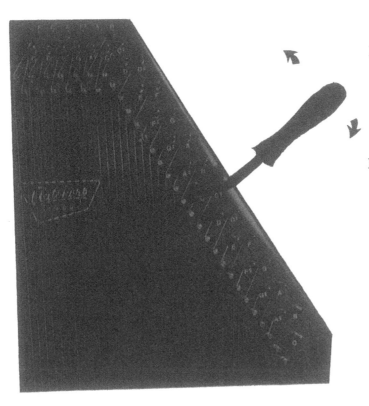

.RECTION FOR LOWERING TONE

IRECTION FOR RAISING TONE

HOLDING

We recommend the Autoharp as a lap instrument, though you may use a table or hold it upright (if you prefer, attach it to a sling held around the neck.)

The long straight side will be next to your body, then turn the right lower corner to rest on your right hip.   (There's no set rule for everybody.   As you go along, you will choose the way most comfortable for you.)

We illus   e various ways of holding the Autoharp:

STROKING

The Autoharp consists of three sections, low (bass), middle and high. Most stroking is across the middle section.

A stroke is a motion over the strings, AWAY FROM THE BODY, using the thumb-nail, hard felt or celluloid pick, or fingernail of the index finger, whichever you find most comfortable.

The LEFT HAND will finger the CHORD BARS.

The RIGHT HAND will stroke the strings.

Press the bars firmly with left hand and stroke from lowest to highest tones (right to left) with the right hand. You may stroke to the right or left of the chord bars, but the left stroke (about 3 inches from the chord bars) will produce a more mellow tone. This will require crossing right hand over left. The right end of the Autoharp is generally used for various strumming effects.

YOU WILL FIND IT MOST COMFORTABLE TO USE ONLY THE MIDDLE THREE FINGERS FOR PRESSING DOWN THE CHORD BARS.

Press and stroke as coincidentally as you can. The chord should be stroked fairly rapidly to coincide with the chord sound.

When a button is depressed, the adjacent strings are silenced. So don't worry about exactly where the stroke stops. Always stroke a few measures as an introduction to the piece you play to set the rhythm and key for singing.

FINGERING THE CHORDS

Chords are preferably pressed with the Index, Middle and Ring Fingers, the guide keys from which all chords are played, like the "touch typing" principle.

INDEX FINGER . . . . On C
MIDDLE FINGER . . . . On G7
RING FINGER . . . . On F

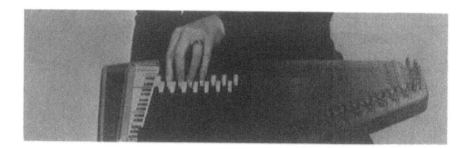

In the pieces which immediately follow, you only need two chords: C and **G7**. Please note that a DIAGONAL LINE / means: Repeat the designated stroke.

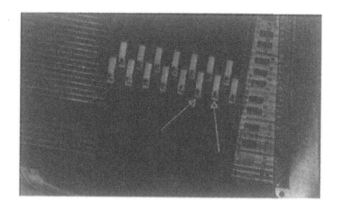

IMPORTANT!   Keep finger firmly on the chord where it extends over one or more notes or (optionally) one or more measures without change.   You need not press the chord every time you see its name or its equivalent diagonal line.

CHORDS: C - G7
COMMENTS: Diagonal line / means "repeat named chord" (see note immediately above)
Diagonal *3* means "triplet" (3 notes take a single count)

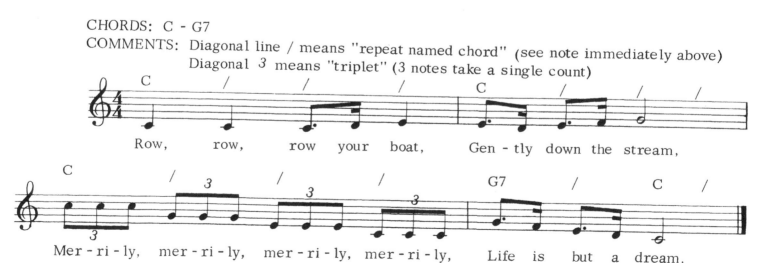

Row,   row,   row   your   boat,   Gen - tly down the   stream,

Mer - ri - ly,   mer - ri - ly,   mer - ri - ly,   mer - ri - ly,   Life   is   but   a dream.

LONDON BRIDGE

CHORDS: C - G7
COMMENT: Note that the last stroke follows the "dy" in "la-dy".

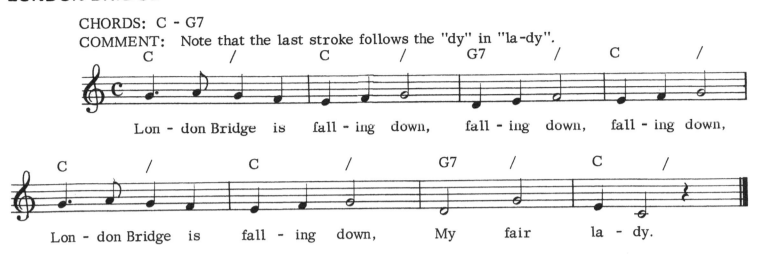

Lon - don Bridge is fall - ing down, fall - ing down, fall - ing down,

Lon - don Bridge is fall - ing down, My fair la - dy.

BROTHER JOHN

CHORDS: C - G7
COMMENT: You may omit the "G7" and play the entire song with the "C" chord.

Are you sleep - ing? Are you sleep - ing? Broth - er John, Broth - er John,

Morn-ing bells are ring - ing, Morn-ing bells are ring - ing, Ding ding dong, Ding ding dong.

THREE BLIND MICE

CHORDS: C - G7
COMMENT: In 6/8 time, each chord gets 3 counts.

Three Blind Mice, Three Blind Mice, See how they run! See how they run!

They ran af - ter the farm - er's wife, She cried to the farm-er: "Oh save my life!" The

farm - er said: "Don't be a - fraid of the nice lit - tle Three Blind Mice."

BILLY BOY

CHORDS: C - G7

Comment: 2/4 time usually requires 2 brisk strokes in each measure. Don't count the opening "Oh", which is just a "pick-up" for starting the piece.

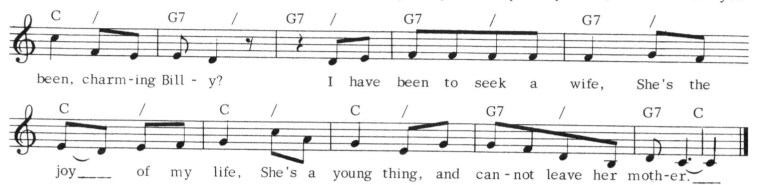

Oh,___ where have you been, Bill-y boy? Bill-y boy? Oh,_ where have you

been, charm-ing Bill-y? I have been to seek a wife, She's the

joy___ of my life, She's a young thing, and can-not leave her moth-er.___

THE BOWERY

CHORDS: C - G7

COMMENT: Use "Waltz Stroke", 3 beats to a measure. Stroke lower third of strings on first beat, lighter stroke on middle strings for 2nd beat, then very light stroke on higher strings.

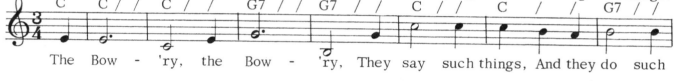

The Bow - 'ry, the Bow - 'ry, They say such things, And they do such

things on the Bow - 'ry, the Bow - 'ry, I'll nev-er go there an-y more._____

SKIP TO MY LOU

CHORDS: C - G7

COMMENT: ₵ is a faster 4/4 than C; 2 brisk strokes to a measure. Vary as indicated.

Lost my part-ner, what-'ll I do? Lost my part-ner, what-'ll I do? Lost my part-ner,

what-'ll I do? Skip to my Lou my dar-lin'. Skip, skip, skip to my Lou,

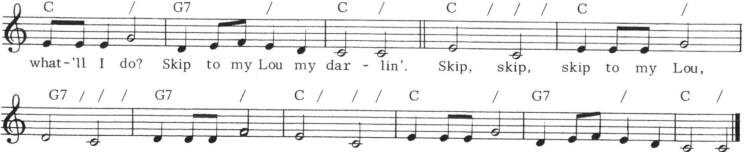

Skip, skip, skip to my Lou, Skip, skip, skip to my Lou, Skip to my Lou, my dar-lin'.

A TISKET, A TASKET

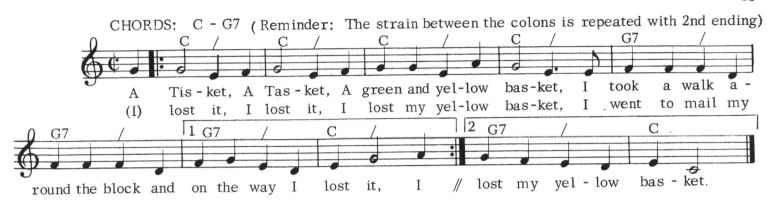

OH, DEAR, WHAT CAN THE MATTER BE?

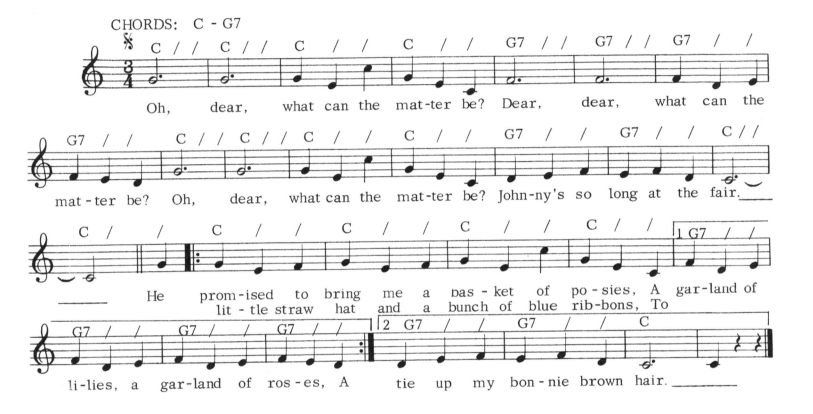

SING A SONG OF SIXPENCE

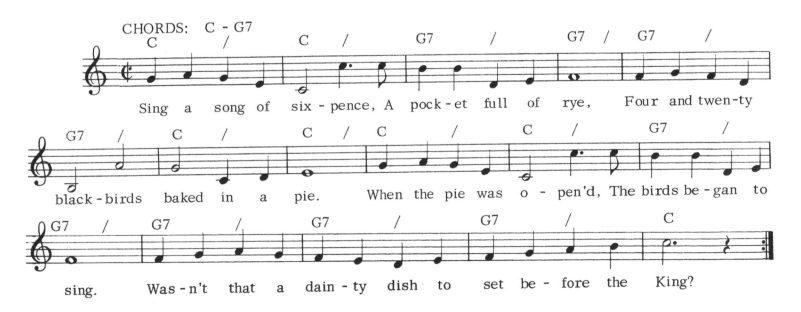

14

Now, let's add C7 and F Chords to the tunes:

MARY HAD A LITTLE LAMB

CHORDS: F - C7

Ma - ry had a lit-tle lamb, lit-tle lamb, lit-tle lamb, Ma - ry had a
ev - 'ry-where that Ma-ry went, Ma-ry went, Ma-ry went, Ev - 'ry-where that

lit-tle lamb, Its fleece was white as snow. And
Ma-ry went, The --- lamb was sure to go.

TEN LITTLE INDIANS

CHORDS: F - C7

1 lit-tle, 2 lit - tle, 3 lit - tle In-dians, 4 lit-tle, 5 lit-tle,

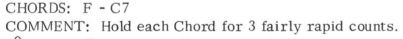

6 lit - tle In-dians, 7 lit-tle, 8 lit-tle, 9 lit-tle In-dians, 10 lit-tle In-dian boys.

THE MULBERRY BUSH

CHORDS: F - C7
COMMENT: Hold each Chord for 3 fairly rapid counts.

Here we go 'round the mul-ber-ry bush, the mul-ber-ry bush, the mul-ber-ry

bush. Here we go 'round the mul-ber-ry bush, So ear - ly in__ the morn - ing.

PICKS

We illustrate various "picks" used by Autoharpists.   Some are plastic, celluloid or felt, attached
to the fingers or held between **thumb and forefinger.** Many prefer to use **the fingernail.**

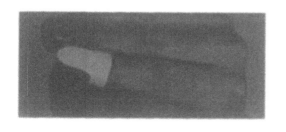

LONG LONG AGO

THOMAS H. BAYLY

CHORDS: F - C7
COMMENT: Play slowly on low and middle strings; 4 even strokes to the measure.

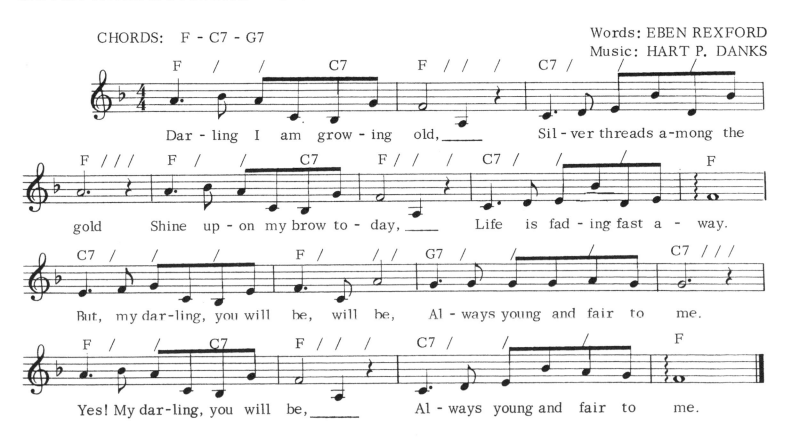

Tell me the tales that to me were so dear, Long long a-go,

Long long a-go. Sing me the songs I de-light-ed to hear,

Long long a-go, long a-go. Now you are come, all my

✻ This is a "glissando" (a full sweep across the strings)

grief is re-mov'd, Let me for-get that so long you have roved.

Let me be-lieve that you love as you loved, Long long a-go, long a-go.

SILVER THREADS AMONG THE GOLD

Words: EBEN REXFORD
Music: HART P. DANKS

CHORDS: F - C7 - G7

Dar-ling I am grow-ing old,____ Sil-ver threads a-mong the

gold Shine up-on my brow to-day,____ Life is fad-ing fast a-way.

But, my dar-ling, you will be, will be, Al-ways young and fair to me.

Yes! My dar-ling, you will be,_____ Al-ways young and fair to me.

THERE IS A TAVERN IN THE TOWN

DOWN IN THE VALLEY

THE MARINES' HYMN

CHORDS: C - G7 - F

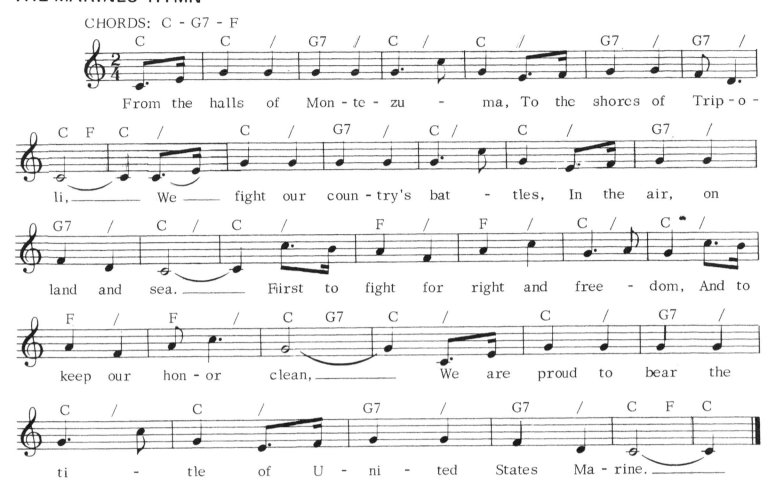

From the halls of Mon - te - zu - ma, To the shores of Trip - o -
li, _____ We _____ fight our coun - try's bat - tles, In the air, on
land and sea. _____ First to fight for right and free - dom, And to
keep our hon - or clean, _____ We are proud to bear the
ti - tle of U - ni - ted States Ma - rine. _____

ON TOP OF OLD SMOKY

CHORDS: C - G7 - F

On Top Of Old Smok - y, _____ All cov-ered with snow, _____
_____ I lost my true lov - er, _____ Came a -court-in' too slow.
A - court -in's a pleas - ure, _____ But part - in's a grief.
A false-heart - ed lov - er _____ Is worse than a thief. _____

We now introduce the B♭ Chord:

ALOHA OE

CHORDS: C7 - F - B♭ (middle strings)   By QUEEN LILIUOKALANI

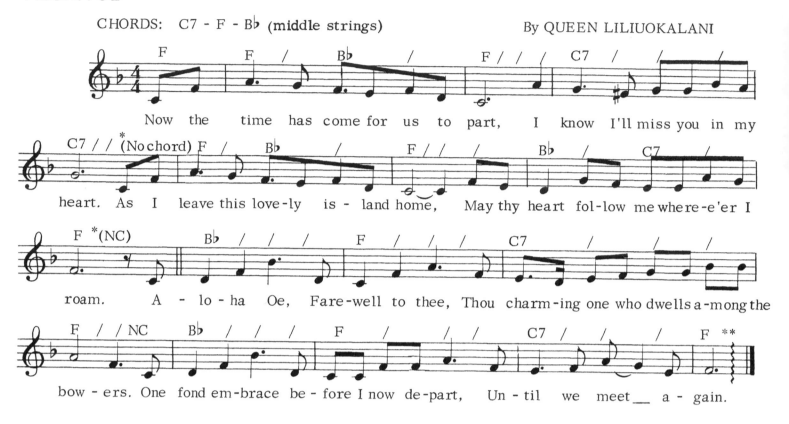

WHEN YOU AND I WERE YOUNG, MAGGIE

CHORDS: C - C7 - F - B♭ - G7 (low and middle strings)   By J. A. BUTTERFIELD

RED RIVER VALLEY

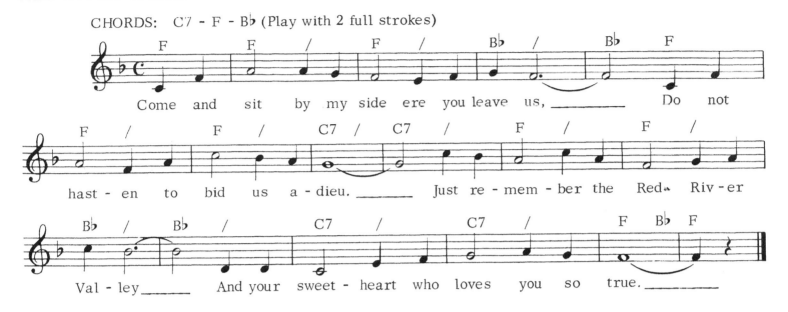

CHORDS: C7 - F - B♭ (Play with 2 full strokes)

Come and sit by my side ere you leave us, _____ Do not hast - en to bid us a - dieu. _____ Just re - mem - ber the Red Riv - er Val - ley _____ And your sweet - heart who loves you so true. _____

HOME ON THE RANGE

CHORDS: C7 - F - B♭

Oh give me a home where the buf - fa - lo roam, Where the deer and the an - te - lope play, _____ Where sel - dom is heard a dis - cour - ag - ing word, And the skies are not cloud - y all day. _____ Home, home on the range, _____ Where the deer and the an - te - lope play, _____ Where sel - dom is heard a dis - cour - ag - ing word, And the skies are not cloud - y all day. _____

OH! SUSANNA

CHORDS: C7 - F - Bb (2 strokes, high strings)

STEPHEN FOSTER

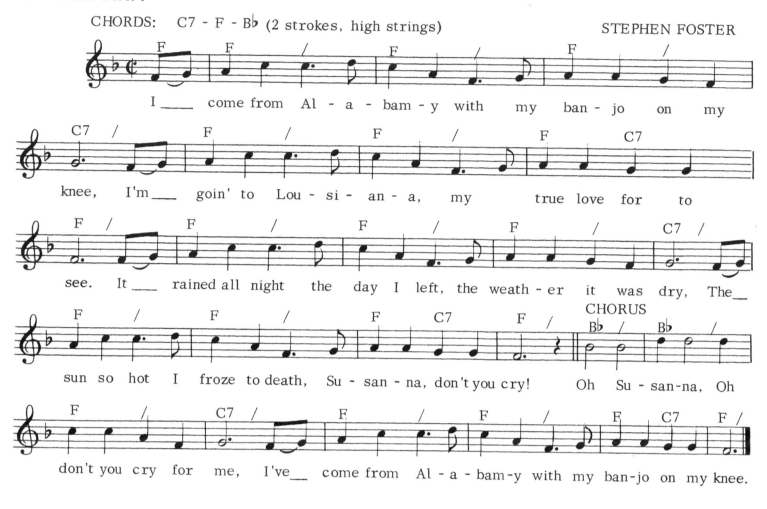

I ___ come from Al - a - bam - y with my ban - jo on my knee, I'm ___ goin' to Lou - si - an - a, my true love for to see. It ___ rained all night the day I left, the weath - er it was dry, The__ sun so hot I froze to death, Su - san - na, don't you cry! Oh Su - san - na, Oh don't you cry for me, I've ___ come from Al - a - bam-y with my ban-jo on my knee.

THE BLUE TAIL FLY

FOLK SONG

CHORDS: C7 - F - Bb (Part I "ad lib"; Part II - 2 short strokes, middle and high strings)

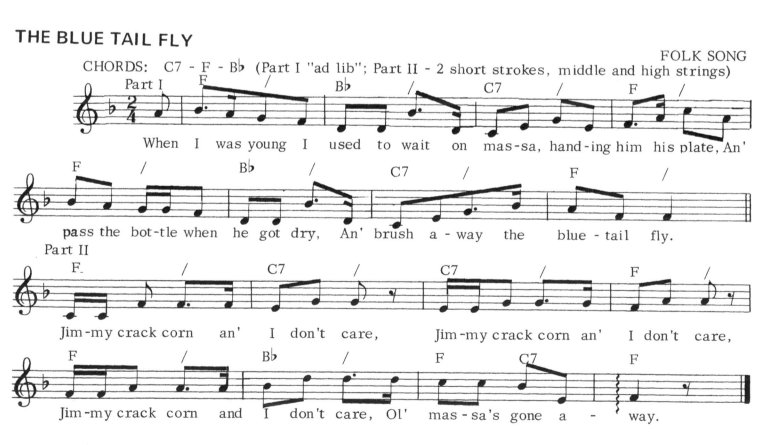

When I was young I used to wait on mas-sa, hand-ing him his plate, An' pass the bot-tle when he got dry, An' brush a - way the blue-tail fly. Jim-my crack corn an' I don't care, Jim-my crack corn an' I don't care, Jim-my crack corn and I don't care, Ol' mas-sa's gone a - way.

FLOW GENTLY, SWEET AFTON

CHORDS: Bb - C7 - F - G7

BURNS - SPILMAN

FOR HE'S A JOLLY GOOD FELLOW

CHORDS: C7 - F - Bb (Note 6/8 time, each stroke for equivalent of 3 - 8th notes)

SILENT NIGHT

CHORDS: C - G7 - F

MOHR-GRUBER

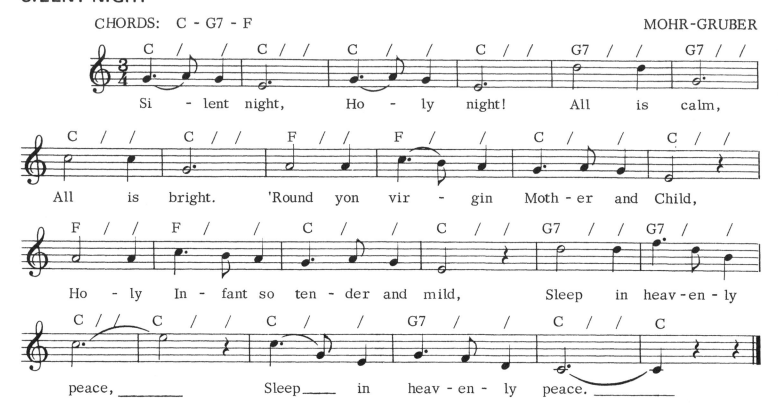

O COME ALL YE FAITHFUL

CHORDS: C - C7 - F - G7 - B♭

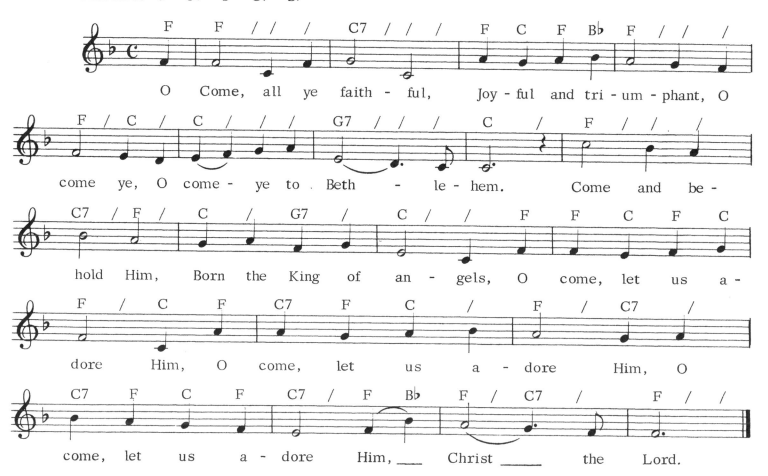

JINGLE BELLS

CHORDS: C7 - F - B♭

Dash-ing thru the snow, In a one horse o-pen sleigh, O'er the fields we go, Laugh-ing all the way. Bells on bob-tail ring, Mak-ing spi-rits bright, What fun it is to ride, and sing a sleigh-ing song to-night!

CHORUS:

Jin-gle bells! Jin-gle bells! Jin-gle all the way. Oh what fun it is to ride in a one horse o-pen sleigh! _____ one horse o-pen sleigh!

DECK THE HALLS

CHORDS: C - C7 - F - G7 - B♭

Deck the halls with boughs of hol-ly, Fa la la la la, la la la la.

'Tis the sea-son to be jol-ly, Fa la la la la, la la la la.

Don we now our gay ap-par-el, Fa la la, Fa la la, La la la.

Troll an an-cient Yule-tide car-ol, Fa la la la la, La la la la.

THE FIRST NOEL

CHORDS: C - F - G7

The— first— No - el, the an-gel did say, Was to cer-tain poor
shep-herds in fields as they lay; In— fields— where— they lay— keep-ing their
sheep, On a cold win-ter's night— that was— so deep. No - el,— No -
el, No - el, No - el, Born is the King— of Is - ra - el.

JOY TO THE WORLD

CHORDS: C - F - G7

GEORGE F. HANDEL

Joy to the world! The Lord is come! Let
earth re - ceive her King. Let ev - 'ry— heart— pre-
pare— Him— room, And Heav'n and na - ture— sing, And—
Heav'n and na - ture— sing, And— Heav - en and
Heav'n— and na - ture sing.

THE TWELVE DAYS OF CHRISTMAS

6th - 12th days:

6 geese a-laying (repeat 5 to 1)

7 swans a-swimming (repeat 6 to 1)

8 maids a-milking (repeat 7 to 1)

9 ladies dancing (repeat 8 to 1)

10 lords a-leaping (repeat 9 to 1)

11 pipers piping (repeat 10 to 1)

12 drummers drumming

   (repeat 11 to 1)

GUANTANAMERA

MARY ANN

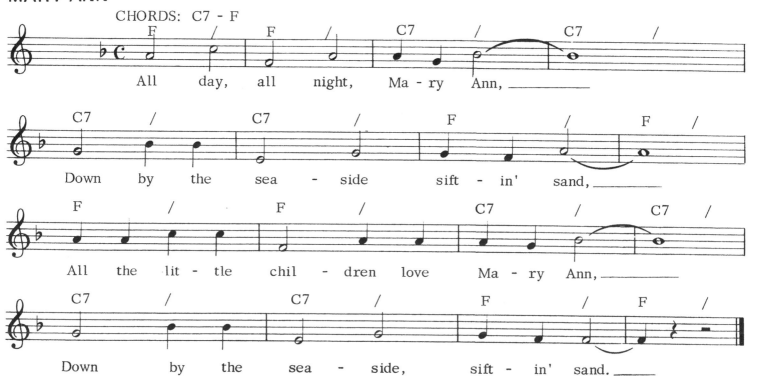

THE RIDDLE SONG

CHORDS: C - F - Bb
COMMENT: Play "ad lib" (as you feel it, not necessarily in strict tempo)

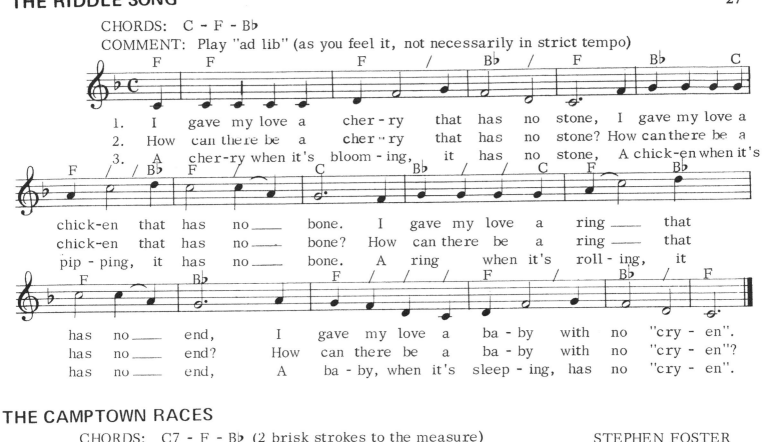

1. I gave my love a cher-ry that has no stone, I gave my love a
2. How can there be a cher-ry that has no stone? How can there be a
3. A cher-ry when it's bloom-ing, it has no stone, A chick-en when it's

chick-en that has no____ bone. I gave my love a ring____ that
chick-en that has no____ bone? How can there be a ring____ that
pip-ping, it has no____ bone. A ring when it's roll-ing, it

has no____ end, I gave my love a ba-by with no "cry-en".
has no____ end? How can there be a ba-by with no "cry-en"?
has no____ end, A ba-by, when it's sleep-ing, has no "cry-en".

THE CAMPTOWN RACES

CHORDS: C7 - F - Bb (2 brisk strokes to the measure)   STEPHEN FOSTER

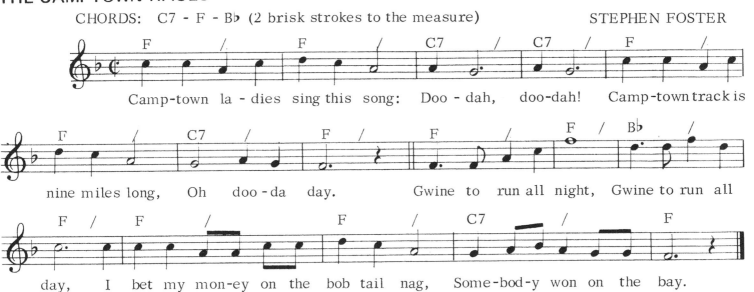

Camp-town la - dies sing this song: Doo - dah, doo-dah! Camp-town track is

nine miles long, Oh doo-da day. Gwine to run all night, Gwine to run all

day, I bet my mon-ey on the bob tail nag, Some-bod-y won on the bay.

LI'L LIZA JANE

CHORDS: C - F - Bb (2 brisk strokes to the measure)

I got a gal in Bal-ti-more, Li'l Li-za Jane! She's the gal that

I a-dore, Li'l Li-za Jane! Oh! E-li-za, Li'l Li-za

Jane! Oh! E-li-za, Li'l Li-za Jane!

STRUMMING

A "strum" differs from a "stroke" in that a "stroke" is a single motion sustaining several notes or an entire measure, whereas a "strum" is played on each beat, like (in 4/4 time) 4 strums to the measure, and sometimes 2 strums to a beat.   The "strums" are played in the approximate areas of the various octaves, the lower, the middle, and the higher octave.

Let's try a typical strumming effect with "DANCE BY THE LIGHT OF THE MOON".

The lower octave will be shown as

The middle octave will be shown as

The higher octave will be shown as

Now, start strumming with a C chord, shifting to G7 as indicated:

DANCE BY THE LIGHT OF THE MOON

CHORDS: C - G7 (4 brisk strums to the measure, in approximate area of octaves indicated)

LITTLE BROWN JUG

CHORDS: C - F - G7

(same strum:) My wife and I live all a-lone in a lit-tle log hut we

call our own. She loves gin and I love rum, I tell you we have

lots of fun. Ha ha ha, you and me, Lit-tle Brown Jug how I love thee!

Ha ha ha, you and me, Lit-tle Brown Jug how I love thee!

In the next piece, we introduce two new chords - D7 and G (found on Autoharps of 12 or more bars).
If you have a 5-bar Autoharp, you can play this piece by substituting C7 and F for these two chords.
The "C" chord in this case will be played as a "Bb" chord.

SHE'LL BE COMIN' 'ROUND THE MOUNTAIN

CHORDS: C - D7 - G

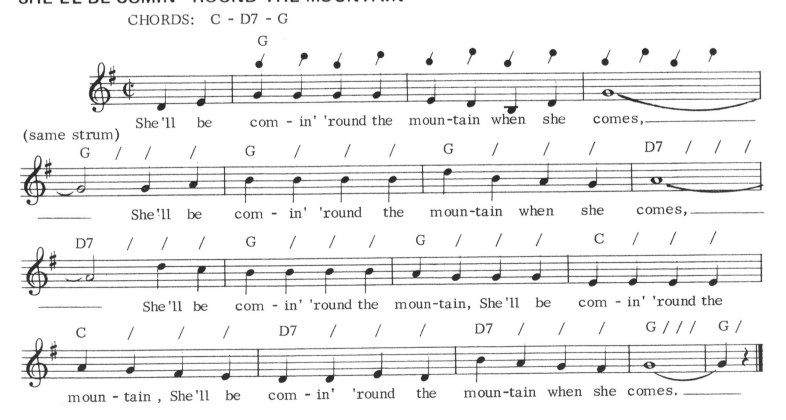

(same strum) She'll be com-in' 'round the moun-tain when she comes,_____

_____ She'll be com-in' 'round the moun-tain when she comes,_____

_____ She'll be com-in' 'round the moun-tain, She'll be com-in' 'round the

moun-tain, She'll be com-in' 'round the moun-tain when she comes. _____

2. She'll be drivin' six white horses when she comes. (Repeat to end)
3. We will all go out to meet her when she comes. (Repeat to end)
4. We'll be singing "Hallelujah" when she comes. (Repeat to end)
5. She'll be puffin' and a-blowin' when she comes. (Repeat to end)

A good "strumming" effect in certain waltzes (with the "oom-pa-pa" beat) is obtained by a stroke in the lower octave for count 1 and two strokes in upper octave for counts 2 and 3. (We introduce "D7")

MY BONNIE

CHORDS: C - D7 - G (for 12-chord Autoharps)
Optional: B♭ - C7 - F (for 5-chord Autoharps)

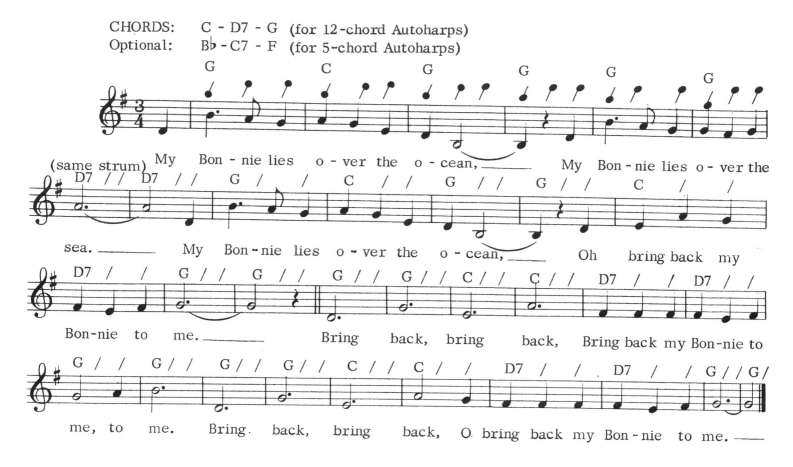

DAISY BELL

CHORDS: B♭ - C7 - F - G7   HARRY DACRE
Reminder: N.C. means "No Chord" played.

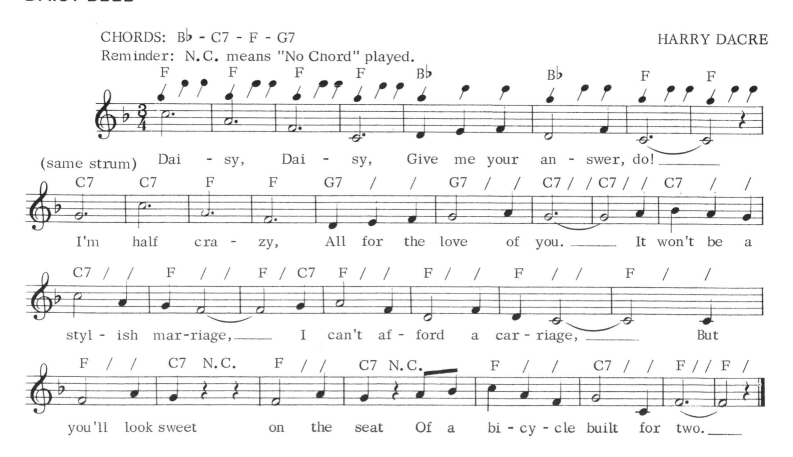

THE SIDEWALKS OF NEW YORK

CHORDS: C7 - F - Bb - G7

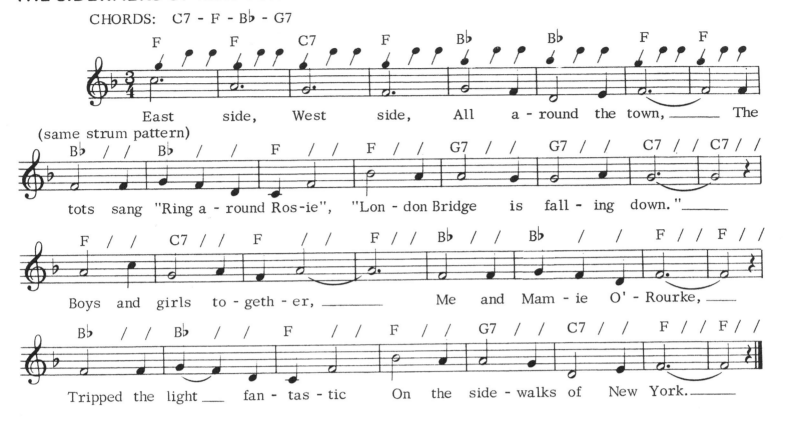

OLD FOLKS AT HOME

STEPHEN FOSTER

Let us try this pattern for an interesting effect.

CHORDS: C - C7 - F - G7

Reminder: Brackets 1 & 2, repeat part between the colons and play #2 second time.

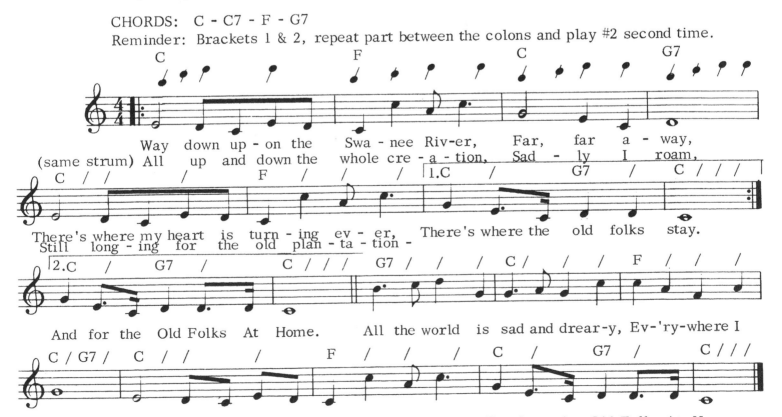

ARPEGGIOS

"Arpeggio" (meaning "like a harp") is a chord passage in which the tones of a chord are played in rapid, even succession.

This effect is produced by a slow stroke in either direction.   We illustrate:

THE UP-STROKE AWAY FROM BODY   THE DOWNSTROKE TOWARD BODY

The UPSTROKE is done with the fleshy part of thumb, the DOWN STROKE with the fleshy part of index finger.   A pick may be used in either case.

In the several illustrative selections which follow, we will designate the ARPEGGIO STROKES like this:

arp   UP STROKE

arp   DOWN STROKE

arp ~~~~~~➤ UP AND DOWN (combined) in tempo but "ad lib"
             as to "time up" or "time down".   When timing is
             more strict for "up" or "down" we show each
             stroke separately.

IN THE GOOD OLD SUMMERTIME

SHIELDS and EVANS

COMIN' THRO' THE RYE

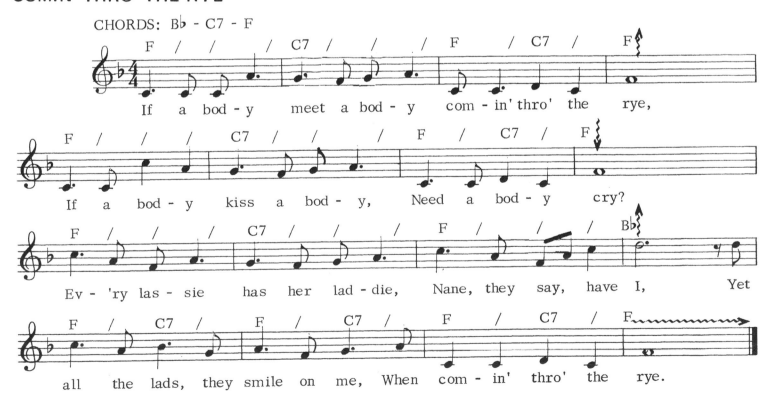

LITTLE ANNIE ROONEY

CHORDS: C - F - G

MICHAEL NOLAN

She's my sweet-heart, I'm her beau.____ She's my An-nie,____ I'm her Joe. Soon we'll mar-ry,____ Nev-er-more to part,____ Lit-tle An-nie Roon-ey ____ is my sweet-heart.____

THE FOGGY FOGGY DEW

Recommended accompaniment: Count 1, regular stroke on lower section; Count 2 - arpeggio.

CHORDS: Bb - C - F - C7

When I was a bach-'lor, I lived all a-lone, I worked at the weav-er's trade,_____ And the on-ly on-ly thing I did that was wrong was to woo a fair young maid.____ I wooed___ her in the win-ter-time,____ And in the sum-mer too,_____ And the on-ly on-ly thing that I did that was wrong, Was to keep her from The Fog-gy Fog-gy Dew.____

KUM–BA–YAH

CHORDS: C - F - G7

NIGERIAN HYMN

2. Hear me crying, Lord, Kum–Ba–Yah! (sing 3 times) .... Oh Lord! Kum–Ba–Yah!
3. Hear me praying, Lord, Kum–Ba–Yah! (sing 3 times) .... Oh Lord! Kum–Ba–Yah!
4. Oh I need you, Lord, Kum–Ba–Yah! (sing 3 times) .... Oh Lord! Kum–Ba–Yah!

JUST A CLOSER WALK WITH THEE

CHORDS: C - F - G7

1. I am weak but Thou art strong. Je - sus,
2. Through this world of toil and snares, If I
3. Just A Clos - er Walk With Thee, Je - sus,

keep me from all wrong. I'll be sat - is - fied as
fal - ter, Lord, who cares? Who with me my bur - den
grant my hum - ble plea! Dai - ly walk - ing close to

long As I walk, let me walk close to Thee.
shares? None but Thee, my dear Lord, none but Thee.
Thee, Let it

be, dear Lord, let it be.

NOTE. - "Arpeggios" will not be shown in the selections which follow. You will use them at your own initiative, preferably when connecting tones which carry over from 6 to 8 beats.

HARMONY PRINCIPLES FOR AUTOHARP

The three most important chords in any key are:

I   THE TONIC (or I) CHORD.   This chord takes the name of the key in which the piece is written.   For instance, if a piece is in the key of F, the Tonic Chord is the F Chord.

IV   THE SUB-DOMINANT (or IV) CHORD.   It is called the IV chord because it features the 4th note of the scale of whatever key is concerned.

V7   THE DOMINANT SEVENTH CHORD, so called because it features the dominant (or 5th) note of the scale plus a flatted 7th note.

Putting this information into practical operation:

In the key of F, the Tonic or I Chord is F (a chord which combines notes F A C)
The Sub-dominant or IV Chord is B♭ (a chord which combines F B♭ D)
The Dominant 7th Chord is C7 (a chord which combines C E G B♭)

The following chart illustrates the I, IV and V7 Chords in all keys in use on the 12-bar Autoharp.   With these three most important chords, in the chosen key, you can accompany most folk songs and many other songs.

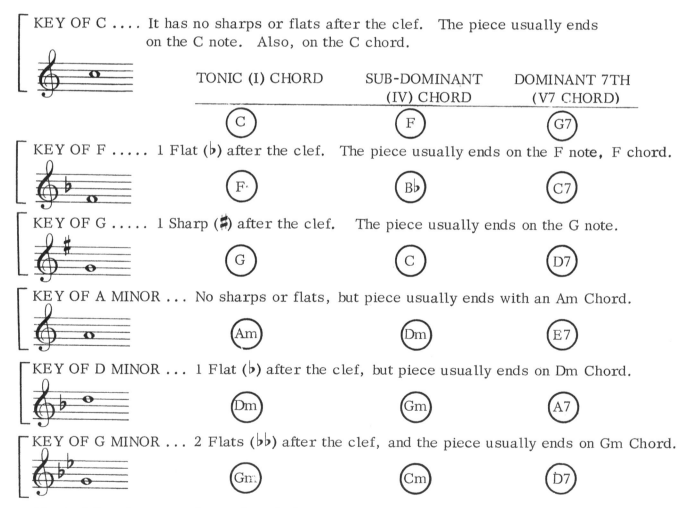

KEY OF C .... It has no sharps or flats after the clef. The piece usually ends on the C note. Also, on the C chord.

TONIC (I) CHORD	SUB-DOMINANT (IV) CHORD	DOMINANT 7TH (V7 CHORD)
C	F	G7

KEY OF F ..... 1 Flat (♭) after the clef. The piece usually ends on the F note, F chord.

| F· | B♭ | C7 |

KEY OF G ..... 1 Sharp (♯) after the clef. The piece usually ends on the G note.

| G | C | D7 |

KEY OF A MINOR ... No sharps or flats, but piece usually ends with an Am Chord.

| Am | Dm | E7 |

KEY OF D MINOR ... 1 Flat (♭) after the clef, but piece usually ends on Dm Chord.

| Dm | Gm | A7 |

KEY OF G MINOR ... 2 Flats (♭♭) after the clef, and the piece usually ends on Gm Chord.

| Gm | Cm | D7 |

Most of the pieces you have already learnt are accompanied by one of the above sets of chords.   They are restricted to the keys C, F and G.   If any of them are not comfortable for your voice, you can experiment by substituting another set of chords, but be sure to do so throughout the entire piece.   A special chapter on TRANSPOSITION will elaborate on this.

RHYTHMS

As you develop your own style, you may vary the rhythmic accompaniments to the way you feel them.

For example, where the sound of a chord continues for a measure or more, you may prefer an "arpeggio" (full sound across the strings) to a group of strokes. Or, you may want to interpret the song rather freely in a manner called the "recitative style".

It is suggested that you stroke two or three measures as an introduction to set the key in which the song will be sung. Many songs start with one or more "pick up" notes before the full rhythm comes into play. These are usually not chorded, so the preliminary strokes will enable you to start singing in the chosen key without the benefit of a chord to guide you.

The most common RHYTHMS will now be discussed:

| 1. 4/4 or C (Common) time. | $\frac{4}{4}$ C ¢ |

This tempo requires 4 beats to a measure. The slower ballads require 2 even strokes to the measure over low and middle strings or 4 even strokes to the measure over the middle strings only. The faster tempo tunes, some of which are marked ¢ (cut time) are played like 2/4 time. The recitative style like in "The Rosary" is effective with sweeping "arpeggios" over all the strings.

| 2. 2/4 time. | $\frac{2}{4}$ |

This tempo requires one sweep gliding evenly over the low and middle strings. For the fast tempos in 2/4 time, try 2 short strokes to the measure, the first over the middle strings, the second over the high strings.

2/4 time, while normally associated with polkas, spirited marches and other quick tempo tunes, is also used for slow tunes like "I Love You Truly" (two medium sweeps to the measure over low and middle strings.)

| 3. 6/8 time. | $\frac{6}{8}$ |

6/8 time is normally played with 2 medium glides to the measure over the low and middle strings for slow tunes like "Believe Me" and "Drink To Me Only". Bright march tunes in 6/8 are treated like the fast tempo 2/4 tunes...2 short strokes over middle and high strings, each stroke taking 3 quick counts.

| 4. 3/4 time. | $\frac{3}{4}$ |

3/4 time requires 3 strokes to the measure, a down beat on low strings with a short stroke, followed by two up beats with short strokes on the middle strings. Optional: Down beat on the middle strings and up beats on the high strings. This tempo is mainly for waltzes.

THE FOLLOWING NEW CHORDS WILL BE FOUND AMONG THE PIECES WHICH FOLLOW:

(m is "minor") **Am   Dm   Gm   A7   E7**

TRANSPOSITION

Songs are usually printed in keys for average voices.   Your range may be higher or lower.
Or the song (outside the ones in this book) may contain many chords unsuited to the Autoharp.
The following will guide you in transposing these songs to your individual needs:

1. See the chart on opposite page.   In heavy borders, you have a choice of 4 possible keys
suitable for the 12-chord Autoharp.   You can tranpose FROM any group of chords on the
chart, but INTO only these 4 keys. (If you own a 15-chord Autoharp, you have 2 additional
means of transposition.

2. Note that tones go higher in sequence: A - B - C - D - E - F - G - A &c

3. Write a line of chords to be transposed.   Under this line, write a new line which contains
in the same columns all or most of the chords you can use (from the keys mentioned above)
Chords useable on the 12-chord Autoharp are circled; additional chords for the 15-chord
Autoharp are in squares.

EXAMPLE "A" - SIDEWALKS OF NEW YORK   Are these tones a bit too high for your voice?

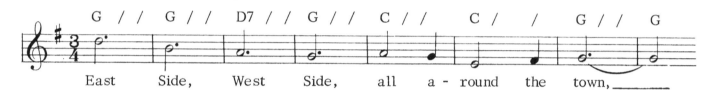

Write down the chords you see: G   D7   C   Note they are in Group XII on the chart.   You
can drop a full tone to the F chords in Group X.   You will readily see that G corresponds to
F in column 1, C corresponds to B♭ in column 6, D7 corresponds to C7 in column 8.   Since
all three of the new chords have circles, you can play them on your Autoharp.   The music
line will now look like this:

EXAMPLE "B" - MARINES' HYMN   It might have been printed with "impossible" chords:

D♭ leads Group VI.   Transpose to Group V, and (instead of D♭, A♭7 and G♭) you will
play C, G7 and F ..... feasible for any Autoharp.   It will now look like this:

NOTE. - The transposed piece may have MOST but not ALL chords playable on your instrument.
Some you may have to mark NC (No Chord) and sing without chord accompaniment.   Too many
NC chords will naturally throw the song out of your range and cannot be used on your Autoharp.

TRANSPOSITION CHART

	1	2	3	4	5	6	7	8	9	10	11	12
GROUP I	Ab / Abm / Ab7	A / Am / A7	Bb / Bbm / Bb7	B / Bm / B7	C / Cm / C7	Db / Dbm / Db7	D / Dm / D7	Eb / Ebm / Eb7	E / Em / E7	F / Fm / F7	Gb / Gbm / Gb7	G / Gm / G7
GROUP II	A / Am / A7	Bb / Bbm / Bb7	B / Bm / B7	C / Cm / C7	Db / Dbm / Db7	D / Dm / D7	Eb / Ebm / Eb7	E / Em / E7	F / Fm / F7	Gb / Gbm / Gb7	G / Gm / G7	Ab / Abm / Ab7
GROUP III ★	Bb / Bbm / Bb7	B / Bm / B7	C / Cm / C7	Db / Dbm / Db7	D / Dm / D7	Eb / Ebm / Eb7	E / Em / E7	F / Fm / F7	Gb / Gbm / Gb7	G / Gm / G7	Ab / Abm / Ab7	A / Am / A7
GROUP IV	B / Bm / B7	C / Cm / C7	Db / Dbm / Db7	D / Dm / D7	Eb / Ebm / Eb7	E / Em / E7	F / Fm / F7	Gb / Gbm / Gb7	G / Gm / G7	Ab / Abm / Ab7	A / Am / A7	Bb / Bbm / Bb7
GROUP V ★	C / Cm / C7	Db / Dbm / Db7	D / Dm / D7	Eb / Ebm / Eb7	E / Em / E7	F / Fm / F7	Gb / Gbm / Gb7	G / Gm / G7	Ab / Abm / Ab7	A / Am / A7	Bb / Bbm / Bb7	B / Bm / B7
GROUP VI	Db / Dbm / Db7	D / Dm / D7	Eb / Ebm / Eb7	E / Em / E7	F / Fm / F7	Gb / Gbm / Gb7	G / Gm / G7	Ab / Abm / Ab7	A / Am / A7	Bb / Bbm / Bb7	B / Bm / B7	C / Cm / C7
GROUP VII ☆	D / Dm / D7	Eb / Ebm / Eb7	E / Em / E7	F / Fm / F7	Gb / Gbm / Gb7	G / Gm / G7	Ab / Abm / Ab7	A / Am / A7	Bb / Bbm / Bb7	B / Bm / B7	C / Cm / C7	Db / Dbm / Db7
GROUP VIII ☆	Eb / Ebm / Eb7	E / Em / E7	F / Fm / F7	Gb / Gbm / Gb7	G / Gm / G7	Ab / Abm / Ab7	A / Am / A7	Bb / Bbm / Bb7	B / Bm / B7	C / Cm / C7	Db / Dbm / Db7	D / Dm / D7
GROUP IX	E / Em / E7	F / Fm / F7	Gb / Gbm / Gb7	G / Gm / G7	Ab / Abm / Ab7	A / Am / A7	Bb / Bbm / Bb7	B / Bm / B7	C / Cm / C7	Db / Dbm / Db7	D / Dm / D7	Eb / Ebm / Eb7
GROUP X ★	F / Fm / F7	Gb / Gbm / Gb7	G / Gm / G7	Ab / Abm / Ab7	A / Am / A7	Bb / Bbm / Bb7	B / Bm / B7	C / Cm / C7	Db / Dbm / Db7	D / Dm / D7	Eb / Ebm / Eb7	E / Em / E7
GROUP XI	Gb / Gbm / Gb7	G / Gm / G7	Ab / Abm / Ab7	A / Am / A7	Bb / Bbm / Bb7	B / Bm / B7	C / Cm / C7	Db / Dbm / Db7	D / Dm / D7	Eb / Ebm / Eb7	E / Em / E7	F / Fm / F7
GROUP XII ★	G / Gm / G7	Ab / Abm / Ab7	A / Am / A7	Bb / Bbm / Bb7	B / Bm / B7	C / Cm / C7	Db / Dbm / Db7	D / Dm / D7	Eb / Ebm / Eb7	E / Em / E7	F / Fm / F7	Gb / Gbm / Gb7

KEY TO CHART:

○   Chords on 12-Chord Autoharp

□   Chords added to 15-Chord Autoharp

   12-Chord Autoharp ... YOU CAN TRANSPOSE ONLY INTO ONE OF THESE FOUR GROUPS

   15-Chord Autoharp ... Additional transposition possibility.

40

I LOVE YOU TRULY

CHORDS: B♭ - C7 - Dm - F - Gm - A7 - E7

CARRIE JACOBS-BOND

I love you tru - ly, tru - ly, dear, Life with its sor - row, Life with its tear, Fades in - to dreams when I feel you are near, For I love you tru - ly, tru - ly, dear. Ah! love, 'tis some - thing to feel your kind hand, Ah! yes, 'tis some - thing by your side to stand. Gone is the sor - row, Gone doubt and fear, For you love me tru - ly, tru - ly, dear.

AULD LANG SYNE

CHORDS: B♭ - C7 - F

ROBERT BURNS

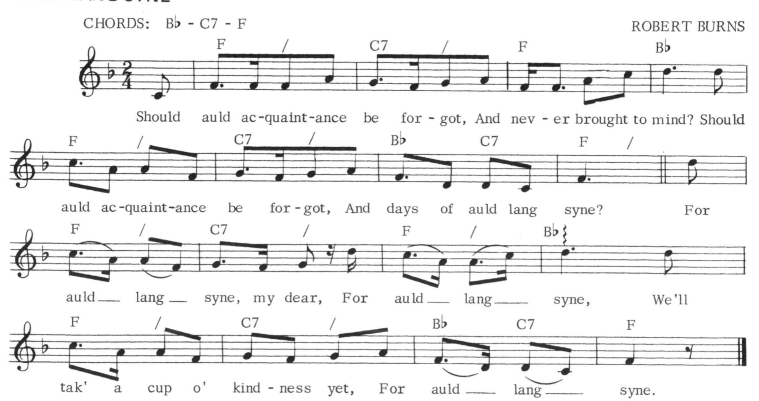

Should auld ac - quaint - ance be for - got, And nev - er brought to mind? Should auld ac - quaint - ance be for - got, And days of auld lang syne? For auld lang syne, my dear, For auld lang syne, We'll tak' a cup o' kind - ness yet, For auld lang syne.

HE'S GOT THE WHOLE WORLD IN HIS HANDS

CHORDS: C7 - F

He's got the whole world ___ in His hands, ___ He's got the
He's got the big sky ___ in His hands, ___ He's got the

whole wide world ___ in His hands, ___ He's got the whole world ___
ti - ny spar-row in His hands, ___ He's got the tall oak trees

in His hands, ___ He's got the whole world in His hands. He's got the
in His hands, ___ He's got the whole world in His hands. And He's got

ti - ny ba - by in His hands, ___ He's got the ti - ny ba - by
you'n me, broth-er, in His hands, ___ And He's got you'n me, sis - ter,

in His hands, ___ He's got the ti - ny ba - by in His hands, ___ He's got the
in His hands, ___ Oh He's got ev - 'ry-bod-y in His hands, ___ He's got the

whole world in His hands, He's got the whole world in His hands. ___
whole world in His hands, He's got the whole world in His hands. ___

MICHAEL (Row The Boat Ashore)

CHORDS: C - Dm - F - G7 (smallest Autoharp substitutes G7 for Dm)

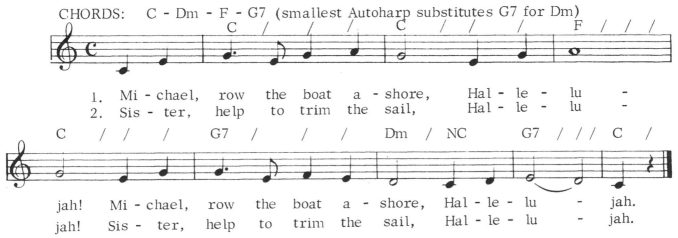

1. Mi - chael, row the boat a - shore, Hal - le - lu -
2. Sis - ter, help to trim the sail, Hal - le - lu -

jah! Mi - chael, row the boat a - shore, Hal - le - lu - jah.
jah! Sis - ter, help to trim the sail, Hal - le - lu - jah.

3. Jordan River is chilly and cold, Hallelujah! Chills the body but not the soul, Hallelujah!
4. Jordan River is deep and wide, Hallelujah! Milk and honey on the other side, Hallelujah!
5. Michael, row the boat ashore, Hallelujah! Michael, row the boat ashore, Hallelujah!

THE BLUE BELLS OF SCOTLAND

CHORDS: C - D7 - F - G7

THE WABASH CANNONBALL

CHORDS: C - G - D7 (2 brisk strokes to the measure)

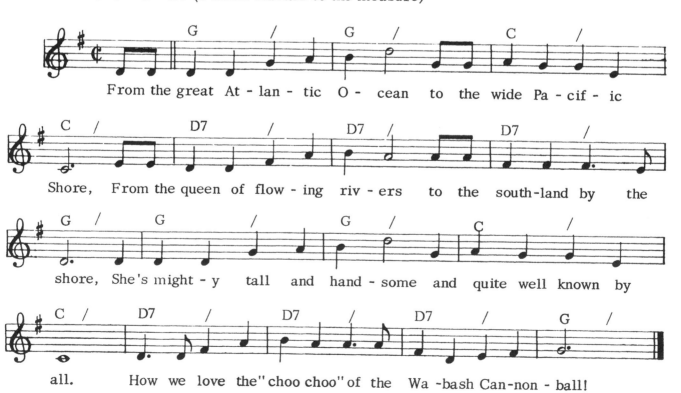

CARRY ME BACK TO OLD VIRGINNY

CHORDS: C - G - D7 - A7

JAMES A. BLAND

AURA LEE

CHORDS: C - G - D7 - A7

FOLK SONG

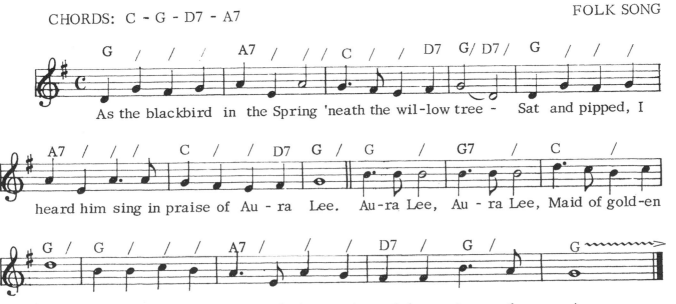

HAIL! HAIL! THE GANG'S ALL HERE

CHORDS: G - D7 (optional: F - C7) - 2 brisk triple-count strokes to the measure.

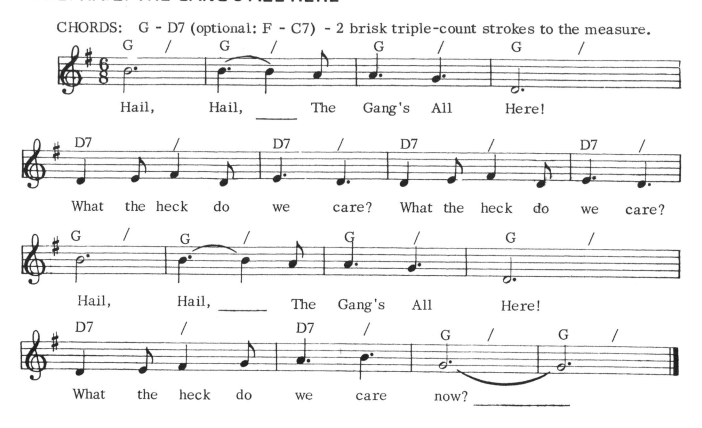

Hail, Hail, _____ The Gang's All Here!

What the heck do we care? What the heck do we care?

Hail, Hail, _____ The Gang's All Here!

What the heck do we care now? _____

MY DARLING CLEMENTINE

CHORDS: G - D7 (optional: F - C7)

1. In a cav - ern in a can - yon, Ex-ca-vat- ing for a mine, Dwelt a

min - er, Fort-y nin - er, And his daught-er, Clem-en-tine. Oh my

dar - ling, oh my dar - ling, Oh my dar - ling Clemen-tine, You are

lost and gone for - ev - er, Dread-ful sor - ry, Clem-en-tine!

2. She drove ducklings to the water,
   Ev'ry morning just at nine,
   Hit her big toe 'gainst a splinter,
   Fell into the foaming brine. (Chorus)

3. Ruby lips above the water,
   Blowing bubbles soft and fine,
   But alas! I was no swimmer,
   So I lost my Clementine. (Chorus)

WHEN YOU WERE SWEET SIXTEEN

WHEN YOU WERE SWEET SIXTEEN

JAMES THORNTON

HELLO! MA BABY

HELLO! MA BABY

JOSEPH HOWARD
IDA EMERSON

NEARER, MY GOD, TO THEE

WERE YOU THERE?

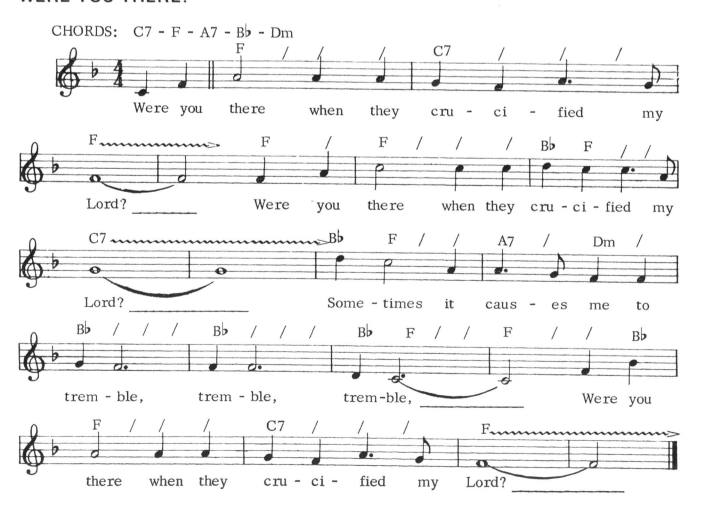

SWING LOW, SWEET CHARIOT

CHORDS: Bb - C - F - G7

Swing Low, Sweet Char - i - ot, ____ Com - in' for to car - ry me home. Swing__ Low, Sweet Char - i - ot, ____ Com - in' for to car - ry me home. Looked o - ver Jor - dan, What did I see? ____ Com - in' for to car - ry me home? A band__ of an - gels com - in' af-ter me, ____ Com-in' for to car - ry me home!

HAND ME DOWN MY WALKING CANE

CHORDS: C - D7 - G - A7 (2 brisk strokes to the measure)

Hand me down ____ my walk - ing cane, ____ Hand me down ____ my walk - ing cane, ____ Hand me down my walk-ing cane, Leav-in' on the mid-night train, All my sins are tak - en a - way. ____

48

LOCH LOMOND

CHORDS: B♭ - C7 - F

SCOTTISH FOLK SONG

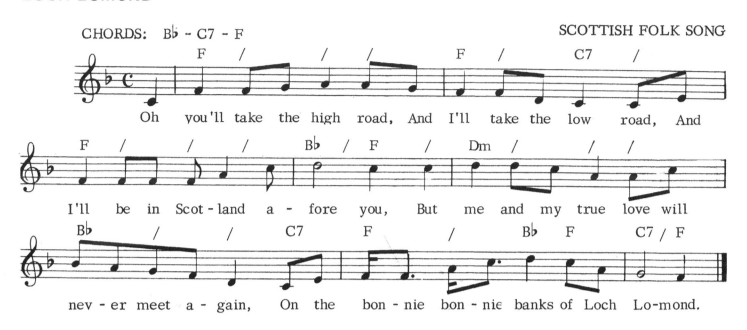

Oh you'll take the high road, And I'll take the low road, And I'll be in Scot-land a - fore you, But me and my true love will nev - er meet a - gain, On the bon - nie bon - nie banks of Loch Lo-mond.

I DREAM OF JEANIE

CHORDS: F - B♭ - C - C7 - A7 - Dm - G7

STEPHEN FOSTER

I dream of Jean - ie with the light, brown - hair, Borne, like a va - por, on the sum-mer air, I see her trip - ping where the bright streams play, Hap- - py as the dai - sies that dance on her way. Man-y were the wild notes her mer-ry voice would pour, Many were the blithe birds that war - bled them o'er, I dream of Jean - ie with the light brown - hair, Float - ing like a va - por on the soft sum - mer air.

THE OLD KENTUCKY HOME

CHORDS: G - C - A7 - D7 (Optional: F - Bb - G7 - C7)

STEPHEN FOSTER

The sun shines bright on the old Ken-tuck-y home, 'Tis sum-mer, the peo-ple are gay. The corn top's ripe and the mead - ow is in bloom, While the birds make mu - sic all the day. The young folks roll on the lit - tle cab - in floor, All mer - ry, all hap - py and bright, By'n by hard times come a - knock-in' at the door, Then my old Ken-tuck-y home, good-night.

REFRAIN: Weep no more, my la-dy, oh weep no more to - day, We will sing one song for the old Ken-tuck-y home, For the old Ken-tuck-y home far a-way.

OLD DOG TRAY

CHORDS: G - D7 (optional: F - C7)

STEPHEN FOSTER

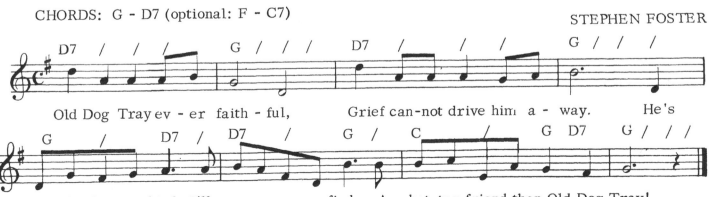

Old Dog Tray ev - er faith - ful, Grief can-not drive him a - way. He's gen-tle, he is kind, I'll nev-er nev - er find - A bet-ter friend than Old Dog Tray!

GIVE MY REGARDS TO BROADWAY

CHORDS: C - Dm - D7 - A7 - G7

GEORGE M. COHAN

MARY'S A GRAND OLD NAME

CHORDS: G - Am - A7 - D7 - E7

GEORGE M. COHAN

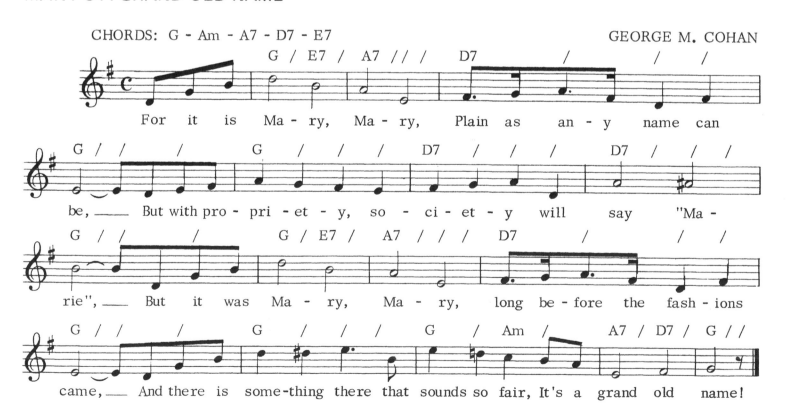

YOU'RE A GRAND OLD FLAG

GEORGE M. COHAN

CHORDS: G - C - D7 - A7 - E7

You're a grand old flag, You're a high fly-ing flag, And for-ev-er in peace may you wave.___ You're the em-blem of the land I love, The home of the free and the brave.___ Ev-'ry heart beats true 'neath the Red, White and Blue, Where there's nev-er a boast or brag,___ But should auld ac-quaint-ance be for-got, Keep your eye on the grand old flag.___

YANKEE DOODLE BOY

GEORGE M. COHAN

CHORDS: C - Dm - D7 - G7 - A7 (2 brisk strokes to measure)

I'm a Yan-kee Doo-dle dan - dy, A Yan-kee Doo-dle, do or die,___ A real live neph-ew of my Un-cle Sam, Born on the Fourth of Ju-ly.___ I've got a Yan-kee Doo-dle sweet - heart, She's my Yan-kee Doo-dle joy. Yan-kee Doo-dle came to Lon-don just to ride the po-nies, I am a Yan-kee Doo-dle boy.___

SWEET MOLLY MALONE

IRISH FOLK SONG

CHORDS: G - D7 - A7

In Dub-lin's fair cit-y, Where girls are so pret-ty, 'Twas there that I first saw sweet Mol-ly Ma-lone, She - drove a wheel-bar-row, Thru streets broad and nar-row, Sing-ing "Cock-les and mus-sels, a-live a-live oh!" A-live, a-live oh ___ , A-live a-live oh! ___ Sing-ing "Cock-les and mus-sels, a-live a-live oh!"

IN THE GLOAMING

META ORRED
ANNIE HARRISON

CHORDS: F - B♭ - C7 - G7

In the gloam-ing, Oh my dar-ling, when the lights are dim and low, And the qui-et shad-ows fall-ing soft-ly come and soft-ly go. Where the winds are sob-bing - faint-ly, with a gen-tle un-known-woe, Will you think of me and love me, As you did once long a-go.

I'LL TAKE YOU HOME AGAIN, KATHLEEN

CHORDS: F - B♭ - C7 - A7 - D7 - G7 - Dm

THOMAS WESTENDORF

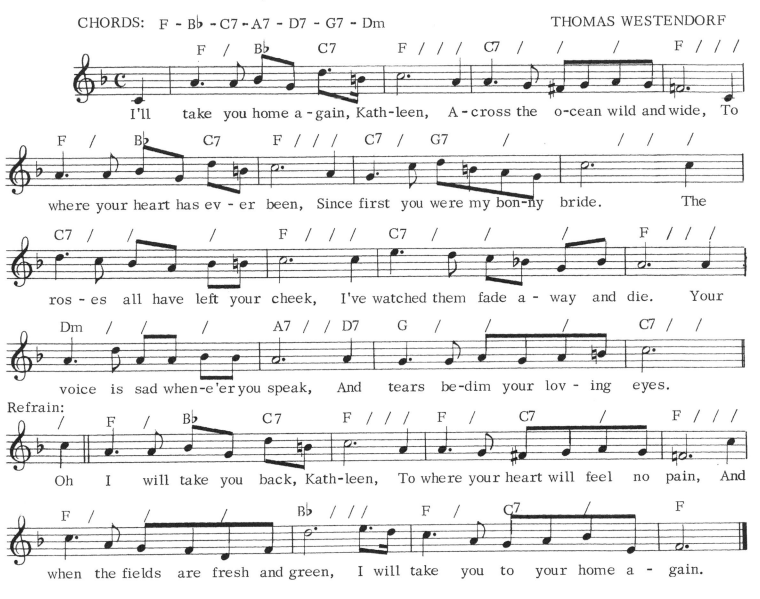

I'll take you home a-gain, Kath-leen, A-cross the o-cean wild and wide, To where your heart has ev-er been, Since first you were my bon-ny bride. The ros-es all have left your cheek, I've watched them fade a-way and die. Your voice is sad when-e'er you speak, And tears be-dim your lov-ing eyes.

Refrain: Oh I will take you back, Kath-leen, To where your heart will feel no pain, And when the fields are fresh and green, I will take you to your home a-gain.

MY GAL SAL

CHORDS: C - C7 - A7 - D7 - E7 - G7 - Am - F

PAUL DRESSER

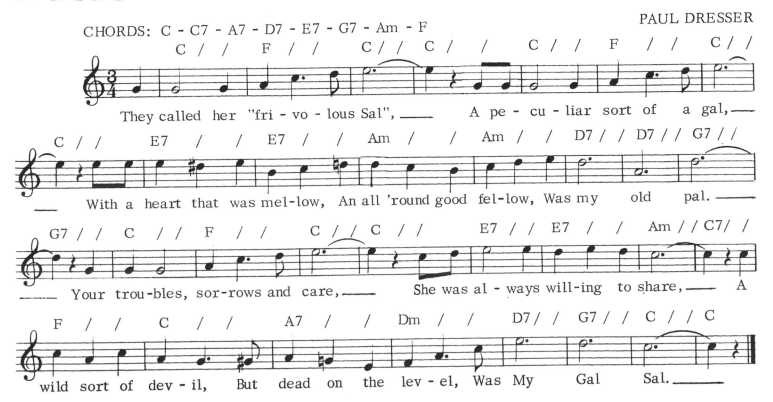

They called her "fri-vo-lous Sal", A pe-cu-liar sort of a gal, With a heart that was mel-low, An all 'round good fel-low, Was my old pal. Your trou-bles, sor-rows and care, She was al-ways will-ing to share, A wild sort of dev-il, But dead on the lev-el, Was My Gal Sal.

LOVE'S OLD SWEET SONG

Suggest: Verse, 2 even strokes to measure, low - middle strings; Refrain, 3 strokes, ending
in a recitative "ad lib" manner.

CHORDS: F - B♭ - C7 - Dm - G7 - A7   BINGHAM and MOLLOY

Once in the dear dead days be-yond re-call,   When on the world the mists be-gan to fall,

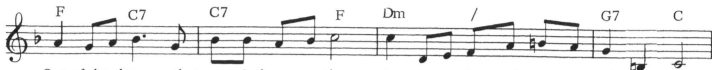

Out of the dreams that rose in hap - py throng, Low to our hearts love sang an old sweet song,

And in the dusk where fell the fire-light's gleam, Soft-ly it wove it-self in - to our dream.

REFRAIN

Just a song at twi-light,   When the lights are low,   And the flick-'ring shad-ows

soft - ly come and go.   Tho' the heart be wear-y,   Sad the day and long,

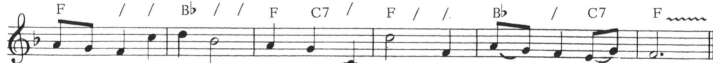

Still to us at twi-light,   Comes love's old song, Comes love's - old sweet - song.

AFTER THE BALL

CHORDS: F - B♭ - C - C7 - D7 - Gm - G7   CHARLES K. HARRIS

Af - ter the ball is o - ver,   Af - ter the break of morn,____

Af - ter the danc - ers' leav - ing,   Af - ter the stars are gone.____

Man - y a heart is ach - ing,   If you could read them all,____

Man-y the hopes that have van - ished, Af - ter the ball!____

BELIEVE ME IF ALL THOSE ENDEARING YOUNG CHARMS

CHORDS: C - F - G7 (stroke on low and middle strings, 2 strokes to the measure - each on count of 3)

THOMAS MOORE

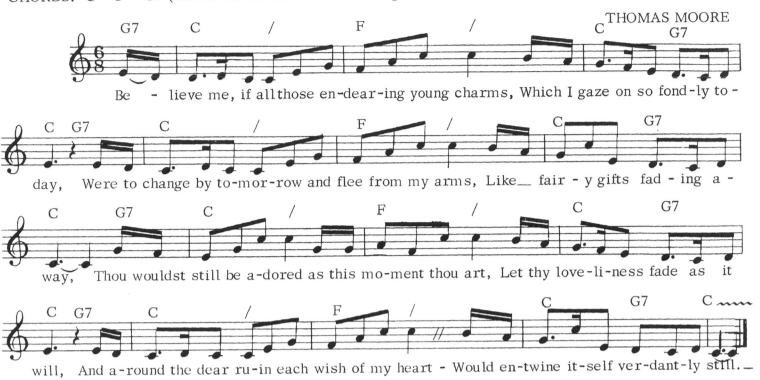

Be - lieve me, if all those en-dear-ing young charms, Which I gaze on so fond-ly to -
day, Were to change by to-mor-row and flee from my arms, Like_ fair - y gifts fad - ing a -
way, Thou wouldst still be a-dored as this mo-ment thou art, Let thy love-li-ness fade as it
will, And a-round the dear ru-in each wish of my heart - Would en-twine it-self ver-dant-ly still._

BEAUTIFUL DREAMER

Comment: 9/8 time is 3 groups of 3/8 time, each group taking a stroke on low and middle strings.

CHORDS: C - F - G - D7 - G7

STEPHEN C. FOSTER

Beau-ti-ful dream-er, wake un-to me, Star-light and dew-drops are wait-ing for
thee._ Sounds of the rude world heard in the day, Lull'd by the moon-light have all passed a -
way._ Beau-ti-ful dream - er, queen of my song, List while I woo thee with
soft mel - o - dy. Gone are the cares of life's bus - y throng,
Beau-ti-ful dream-er, a - wake un-to me.__ Beau-ti-ful dream-er, a - wake un-to me._

GOOD—NIGHT, LADIES

CHORDS: C - G - D7 - G7

Good - night, La-dies! __ Good - night, La-dies! __

Good - night, La-dies! __ We're goin' to leave you now.

Mer - ri - ly we roll a - long, roll a - long, roll a - long,

Mer - ri - ly we roll a - long, O'er the deep blue sea.

GOOD—BYE, MY LOVER, GOOD—BYE

CHORDS: C - G - D7

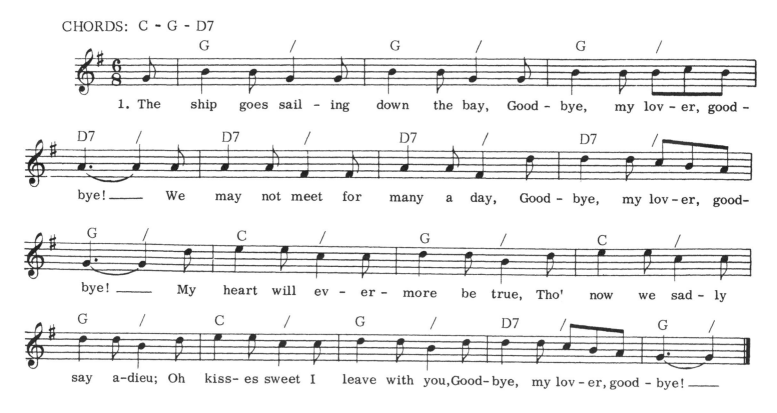

1. The ship goes sail - ing down the bay, Good - bye, my lov - er, good -

bye! __ We may not meet for many a day, Good - bye, my lov - er, good-

bye! __ My heart will ev - er - more be true, Tho' now we sad - ly

say a-dieu; Oh kiss- es sweet I leave with you, Good-bye, my lov - er, good - bye! __

2. I'll miss you on the stormy deep,
   Good-bye, my lover, good-bye!
   What can I do but ever weep?
   Good-bye, my lover, good-bye!
   My heart is broken with regret,
   But never dream that I'll forget;
   I loved you once, I love you yet,
   Good-bye, my lover, good-bye!

3. Then cheer up till we meet again,
   Good-bye, my lover, good-bye!
   I'll try to bear my weary pain,
   Good-bye, my lover, good-bye!
   Tho' far I roam across the sea,
   My ev'ry thought of you shall be;
   Oh, say you'll sometimes think of me,
   Good-bye, my lover, good-bye!

BURY ME NOT ON THE LONE PRAIRIE

CHORDS: G - C - D7

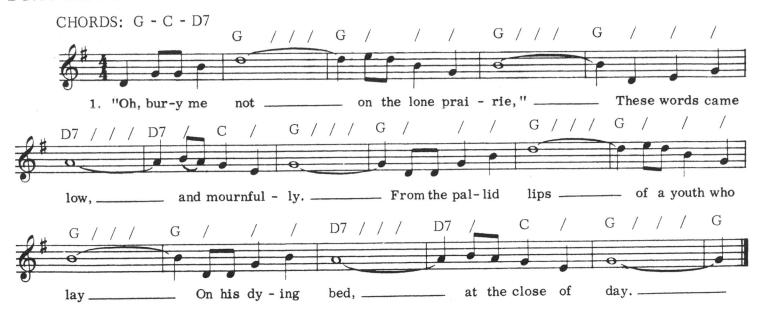

1. "Oh, bur-y me not _____ on the lone prai - rie," _____ These words came low, _____ and mournful - ly. _____ From the pal-lid lips _____ of a youth who lay _____ On his dy - ing bed, _____ at the close of day. _____

2. Oh bury me not on the lone prairie,
   Where the coyotes howl, and the wind blows free.
   In a narrow grave just six by three,
   Oh bury me not on the lone prairie.

3. "Oh bury me not", and his voice failed there,
   But we took no heed of his dying prayer.
   In a narrow grave, just six by three,
   We buried him there on the lone prairie.

4. Yes, we buried him there on the lone prairie,
   Where the owl all night hoots mournfully,
   And the blizzard beats and the wind blows free,
   O'er his lonely grave on the lone prairie.

THE STREETS OF LAREDO

CHORDS: F - C7 - G7 - Dm - Gm

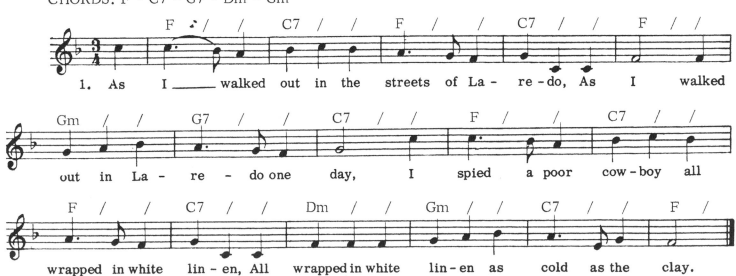

1. As I _____ walked out in the streets of La - re - do, As I walked out in La - re - do one day, I spied a poor cow-boy all wrapped in white lin - en, All wrapped in white lin - en as cold as the clay.

2. "I see by your outfit that you are a cowboy,"
   These words he did say as I boldly stepped by;
   "Come sit down beside me and hear my sad story;
   I was shot in the breast and I know I must die."

3. "It was once in the saddle I used to go dashing,
   It was once in the saddle I used to be gay;
   First to the dram-house and then to the card-house;
   Got shot in the breast and I'm dying today.

4. "Go fetch me some water, a cup of cold water
   To cool my parched lips," the poor cowboy said;
   Before I returned, his spirit had left him,
   No one could revive him; the cowboy was dead.

5. We carried him out to a lovely green valley,
   And there dug a grave by the afternoon light;
   And now when I walk on the streets of Laredo
   I think of the cowboy in linen so white.

58

GREEN GROW THE LILACS

CHORDS: G - C - A7 - D7 - G7

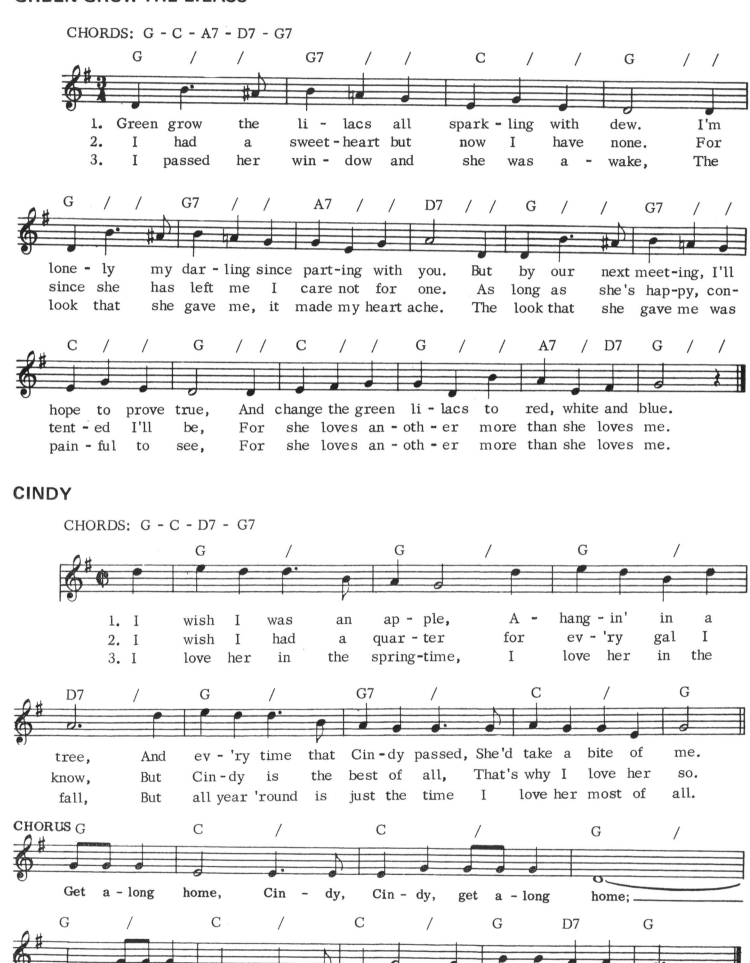

1. Green grow the li - lacs all spark - ling with dew. I'm
2. I had a sweet - heart but now I have none. For
3. I passed her win - dow and she was a - wake, The

lone - ly my dar - ling since part-ing with you. But by our next meet-ing, I'll
since she has left me I care not for one. As long as she's hap-py, con-
look that she gave me, it made my heart ache. The look that she gave me was

hope to prove true, And change the green li - lacs to red, white and blue.
tent - ed I'll be, For she loves an - oth - er more than she loves me.
pain - ful to see, For she loves an - oth - er more than she loves me.

CINDY

CHORDS: G - C - D7 - G7

1. I wish I was an ap - ple, A - hang - in' in a
2. I wish I had a quar - ter for ev - 'ry gal I
3. I love her in the spring-time, I love her in the

tree, And ev - 'ry time that Cin - dy passed, She'd take a bite of me.
know, But Cin - dy is the best of all, That's why I love her so.
fall, But all year 'round is just the time I love her most of all.

CHORUS

Get a - long home, Cin - dy, Cin - dy, get a - long home;

Get a - long home, Cin - dy, Cin - dy, I'll mar - ry you some time.

POLLY WOLLY DOODLE

CHORDS: F - B♭ - C7

ST. JAMES INFIRMARY

CHORDS: Dm - Gm - A7 - B♭

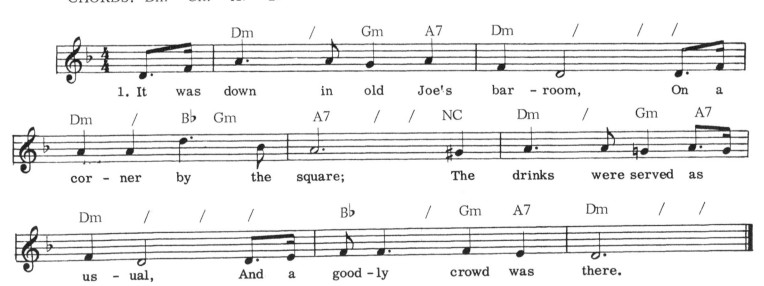

2. On my left stood Joe McKenny
His eyes bloodshot and red,
He gazed at the crowds around him,
And these were the words he said:

3. As I passed St. James Infirmary,
I saw my sweetheart there,
All stretched out on a table,
So pale, so cold, so fair.

4. Sixteen coal-black horses,
Hitched to a rubber-tired hack,
Carried seven girls to the graveyard,
Only six of 'em came back.

5. And now you've heard my story,
I'll take another shot of booze,
If anyone happens to ask you,
Then I've got those gambler's blues.

THE MIDNIGHT SPECIAL

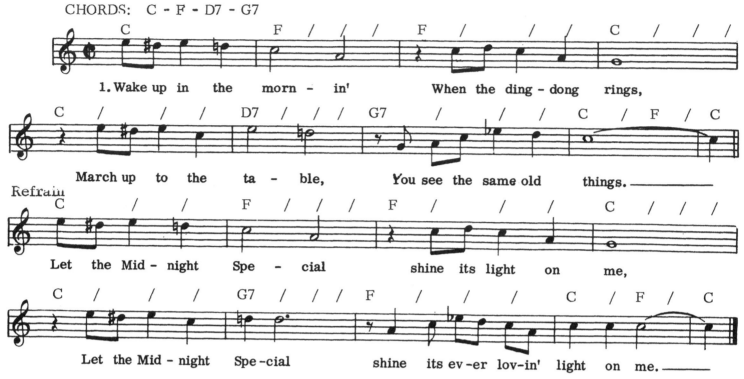

CHORDS: C - F - D7 - G7

1. Wake up in the morn - in' When the ding - dong rings,

March up to the ta - ble, You see the same old things. ____

Refrain

Let the Mid - night Spe - cial shine its light on me,

Let the Mid - night Spe - cial shine its ev - er lov - in' light on me. ____

2. There upon the table,
Knife and fork and pan,
Say a word about it,
There's trouble with the man.
(Refrain)

3. If you go to Houston,
Careful you walk right;
Don't you start no trouble,
And don't get in no fight.
(Refrain)

4. If the cop arrest you,
Judge will send you down;
Jury finds you guilty,
And you are jail-house bound.
(Refrain)

SAILING, SAILING

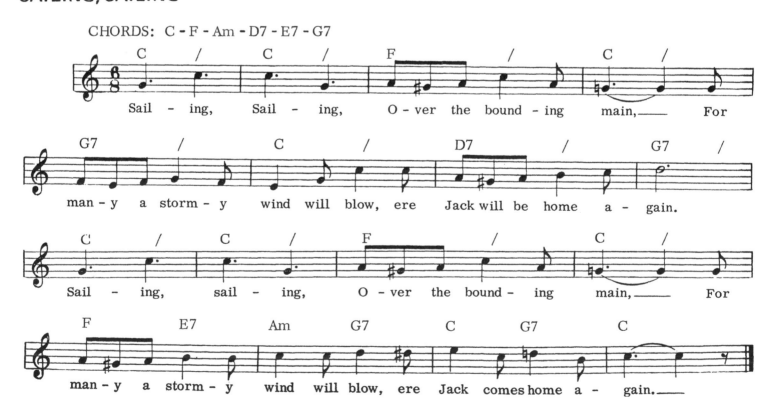

CHORDS: C - F - Am - D7 - E7 - G7

Sail - ing, Sail - ing, O - ver the bound - ing main, ____ For

man - y a storm - y wind will blow, ere Jack will be home a - gain.

Sail - ing, sail - ing, O - ver the bound - ing main, ____ For

man - y a storm - y wind will blow, ere Jack comes home a - gain. ____

THE CRAWDAD SONG

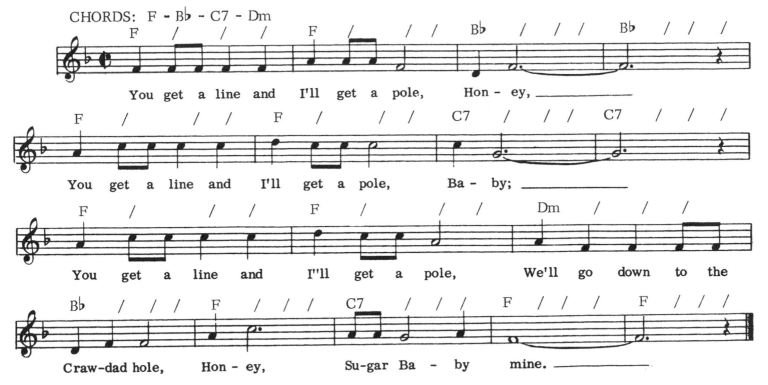

2. What'll you do if the creek goes dry, Honey?
   What'll you do if the creek goes dry, Baby?
   What'll you do if the creek goes dry?
   Just sit down on the bank and cry,
   Honey, Sugar Baby mine.

3. What'll you do when I'm old and gray, Honey?
   What'll you do when I'm old and gray, Baby?
   What'll you do when I'm old and gray?
   Say, "Old man, please stay away,"
   Honey, Sugar Baby mine.

SHORTNIN' BREAD

CORRINA, CORRINA

CHORDS: G - C - C7 - D7

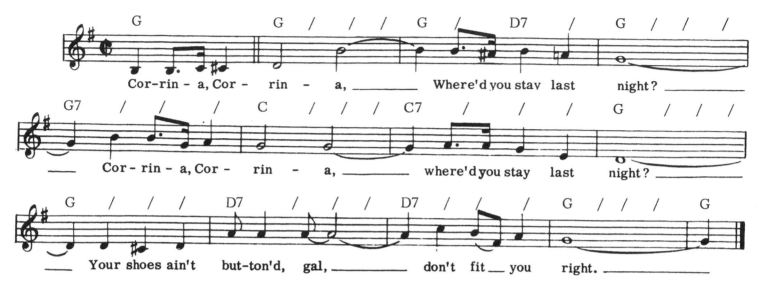

Cor-rin-a, Cor-rin-a, _____ Where'd you stay last night? _____

_____ Cor-rin-a, Cor-rin-a, _____ where'd you stay last night? _____

_____ Your shoes ain't but-ton'd, gal, _____ don't fit _ you right. _____

2. Corrina, Corrina, where've you been so long?
   Corrina, Corrina, where've you been so long?
   Ain't had no lovin', dear, since you have been gone.

3. Corrina, Corrina, what's the matter now?
   Corrina, Corrina, what's the matter now?
   You done gone bad, my babe, which ain't good nohow.

4. Corrina, Corrina, love you, deed I do,
   I love you Corrina, the Good Lord knows I do —
   And I keep hoping, babe, that you love me too.

A—ROVING

CHORDS: F - C - Bb - C7 - Gm

In Am-ster-dam there lived a maid, Mark well what I do say! In

Am-ster-dam there lived a maid, a mis-tress of _ her trade, In Am-ster-dam there

lived a maid, And she was mis-tress_ of her trade, I'll go no more a-

rov-ing with you, fair maid. A-rov-ing, a-rov-ing, Since rov-ing's been my

ru-u-in, I'll go no more a-rov-ing with you, fair maid!

FRANKIE AND JOHNNY

63

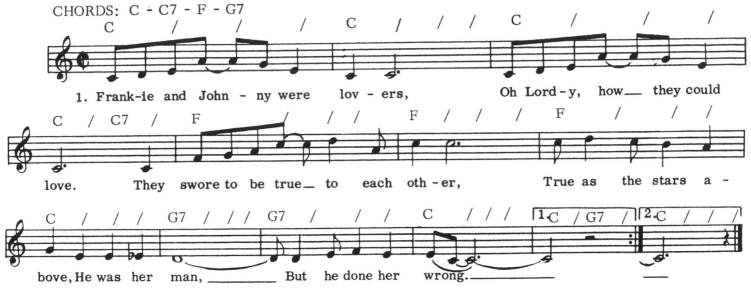

CHORDS: C - C7 - F - G7

1. Frank-ie and John - ny were lov - ers, Oh Lord-y, how__ they could love. They swore to be true__ to each oth-er, True as the stars a-bove, He was her man, _____ But he done her wrong.____

2. Frankie went down to the hotel,
   Looked in the window so high,
   There she saw her lovin' Johnny -
   Make love to Alice Bly,
   He was her man but he done her wrong.

3. Johnny saw Frankie a-comin',
   Down the back stairs he did scoot,
   Frankie - she took out her pistol,
   Boy! How that gal could shoot,
   He was her man but he done her wrong.

4. Frankie, she said to the warden,
   What are they going to do?
   Warden replied, sorry Frankie,
   It's the 'lectric chair for you,
   You shot your man tho' he did you wrong.

5. Frankie, she went to the big chair,
   Calm as a lady could be,
   Turning her eyes up, she whisper'd -
   Lord, I'm coming up to Thee,
   He was my man, but he done me wrong.

THE ROVING GAMBLER

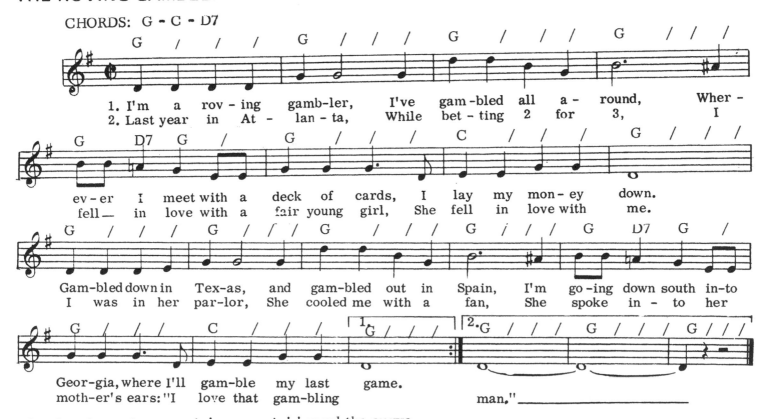

CHORDS: G - C - D7

1. I'm a rov-ing gamb-ler, I've gam-bled all a-round, Wher-ev-er I meet with a deck of cards, I lay my mon-ey down. Gam-bled down in Tex-as, and gam-bled out in Spain, I'm go-ing down south in-to Geor-gia, where I'll gam-ble my last game.

2. Last year in At-lan-ta, While bet-ting 2 for 3, I fell__ in love with a fair young girl, She fell in love with me. I was in her par-lor, She cooled me with a fan, She spoke in-to her moth-er's ears:"I love that gam-bling man."____

3. See the train a-comin', a-comin' 'round the curve,
   A-whistlin' and a-blowin' and a-strainin' ev-'ry nerve.
   Mother, dearest mother, I'll tell you if I can,
   If ever you see me comin' back, it'll be with the gambling man.

THE BOLL WEEVIL SONG

CHORDS: G - D7

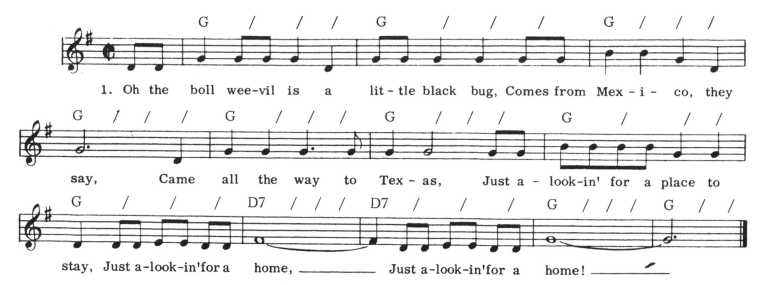

1. Oh the boll wee-vil is a lit-tle black bug, Comes from Mex-i-co, they say, Came all the way to Tex-as, Just a-look-in' for a place to stay, Just a-look-in'for a home, _____ Just a-look-in'for a home! _____

2. The first time I saw the boll weevil,
He was settin' on the square,
The next time I saw the boll weevil,
He had his whole family there,
Just a-lookin' for a home (repeat).

3. The farmer took the boll weevil,
And he put him in hot sand,
The weevil said, this is mighty hot
But I'll stand it like a man,
Gotta have a home! Gotta have a home.

4. The farmer said to the merchant,
We's in an awful fix,
The boll weevil et de cotton up,
And left us only sticks,
Now we got no home, we got no home!

JOHN HENRY

CHORDS: C - F - G - Am

1. John _ Hen - ry said _ to the cap - tain, "A _ man ain't noth-ing but a man, And be - fore I'll let your steam drill beat me down, Die _ with the ham-mer in my hand, O Lord! Die _ with the ham-mer in my hand!

2. John Henry got a thirty pound hammer,
Beside the steam drill he did stand,
He beat that steam drill three inches down,
And died with his hammer in his hand, O Lord!
Died with the hammer in his hand.

3. John Henry had a handsome little son,
Sittin' in the palm of his hand,
He hugged and kissed him and bid him farewell,
Saying "Son, always do the best you can, O Lord!
Always do the best you can."

4. John Henry went straight to the graveyard,
And they buried him in the sand,
And ev'ry locomotive come roarin' by—
There lays a steel-drivin' man, O Lord!
There lays a steel-drivin' man.

LONDONDERRY AIR

OH PROMISE ME

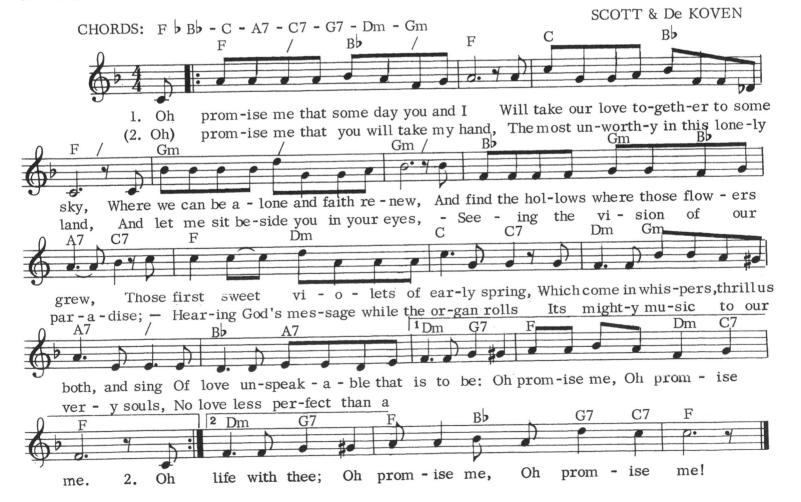

GREENSLEEVES

CHORDS: Dm - C - F - A7 (low and middle strings)

ENGLISH FOLK SONG

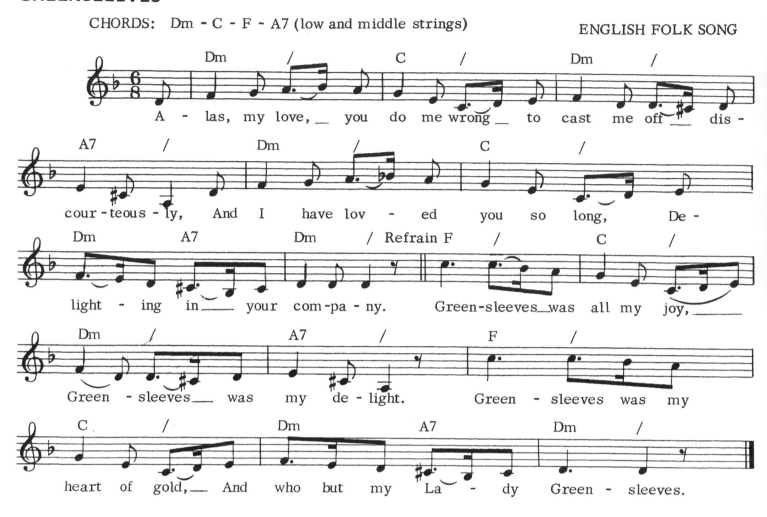

A - las, my love,__ you do me wrong__ to cast me off__ dis-
cour-teous-ly, And I have lov - ed you so long, De-
light - ing in__ your com-pa - ny. Green-sleeves__ was all my joy,__
Green - sleeves__ was my de - light. Green - sleeves was my
heart of gold,__ And who but my La - dy Green - sleeves.

BLACK IS THE COLOR OF MY TRUE LOVE'S HAIR

CHORDS: Dm - Gm - C - C7

FOLK SONG

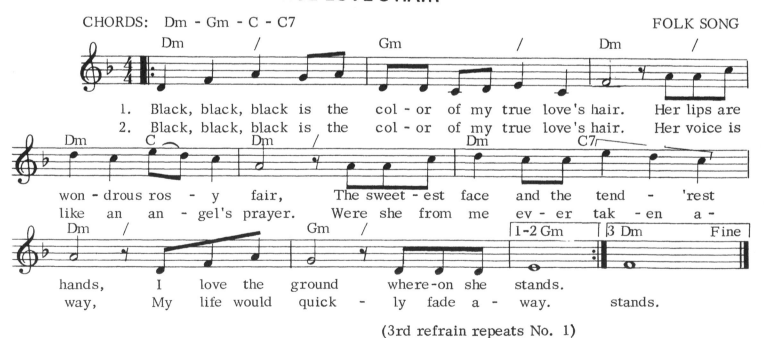

1. Black, black, black is the col - or of my true love's hair. Her lips are
2. Black, black, black is the col - or of my true love's hair. Her voice is

won - drous ros - y fair, The sweet - est face and the tend - 'rest
like an an - gel's prayer. Were she from me ev - er tak - en a -

hands, I love the ground where-on she stands.
way, My life would quick - ly fade a - way. stands.

(3rd refrain repeats No. 1)

OH! THEM GOLDEN SLIPPERS

JAMES A. BLAND

Oh, my gold - en slip-pers are a - laid a - way, 'Cause I will not wear 'em till my

wed-ding day, And my long tail coat that I loved so well, I will wear that cer-tain morn.

CHORUS:

Oh! Them gold-en slip - pers, Oh! Them gold-en slip - pers, Gold-en slip-pers

I will wear, be - cause they look so neat. Oh! Them gold - en slip -pers,

Oh! Them gold-en slip -pers, Gold-en slip-pers I will wear, To walk the gold-en street!

THIS TRAIN

1. This train is bound for glo - ry, this train, _____

This train is bound for glo-ry, this train, _____ This train is

bound for glo - ry, Don't ride none but the good and ho - ly,

This train is bound for glo - ry, this train. _____

2. This train don't carry gamblers, this train,
This train don't carry gamblers, this train,
This train is bound for glory,
Don't ride none but the good and holy,
This train don't carry gamblers, this train.

3. This train don't carry liars, this train,
This train don't carry liars, this train,
This train is bound for glory,
Don't ride none but the good and holy,
This train don't carry liars, this train.

STANDING IN THE NEED OF PRAYER

JOSHUA FIT THE BATTLE OF JERICHO

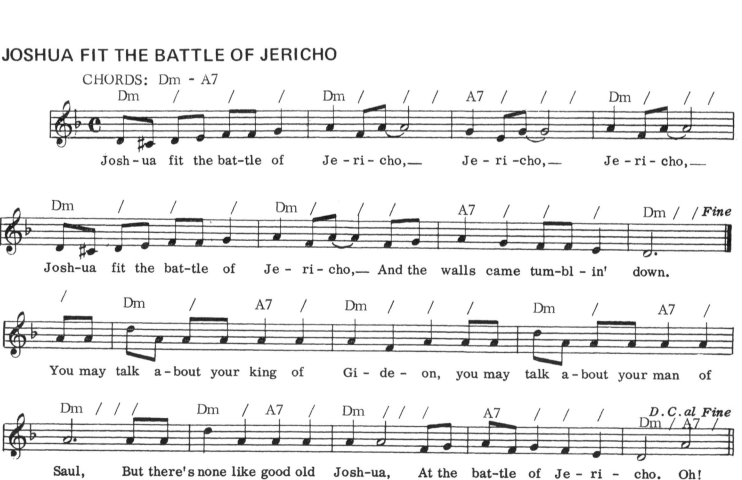

GO TELL IT ON THE MOUNTAIN

CHORDS: G - C - A7 - D7 - G7

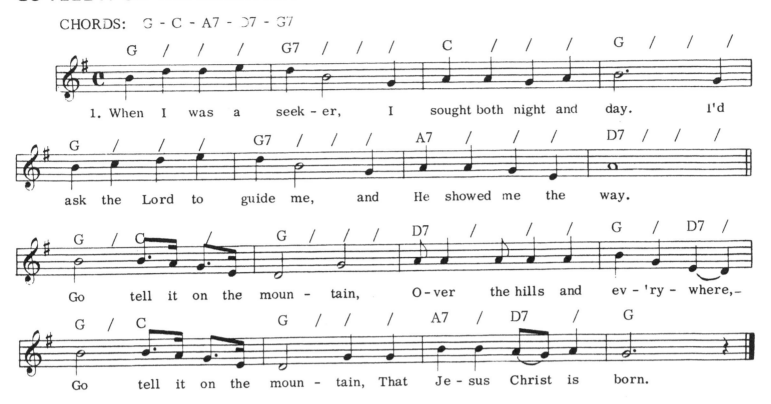

1. When I was a seek - er, I sought both night and day. I'd ask the Lord to guide me, and He showed me the way. Go tell it on the moun - tain, O - ver the hills and ev - 'ry - where,— Go tell it on the moun - tain, That Je - sus Christ is born.

2. While at night the shepherds
   Kept watching near and far,
   They saw that from the Heavens,
   There came a holy star. (Refrain)

3. When the shepherds saw it,
   They wondered and they prayed.
   Then they all went together
   To where the Child was laid.

GIVE ME THAT OLD TIME RELIGION

CHORDS: G - D7 - G7

Give me that old time re - lig - ion, Give me that old time re - lig-ion, Give me that old time re - lig - ion, It's good e-nough for me.

1. It was good for the He - brew chil-dren, It was good for the He - brew chil-dren, It was good for the He - brew chil-dren, And it's good e - nough for me!

2. It will do when the world's on fi - re, It will do when the world's on fi - re, It will do when the world's on fi - re, And it's good e - nough for me!

THE ROSE OF TRALEE

CHORDS: C - F - D7 - G7 - E7 - Am - Dm

SPENCER and GLOVER

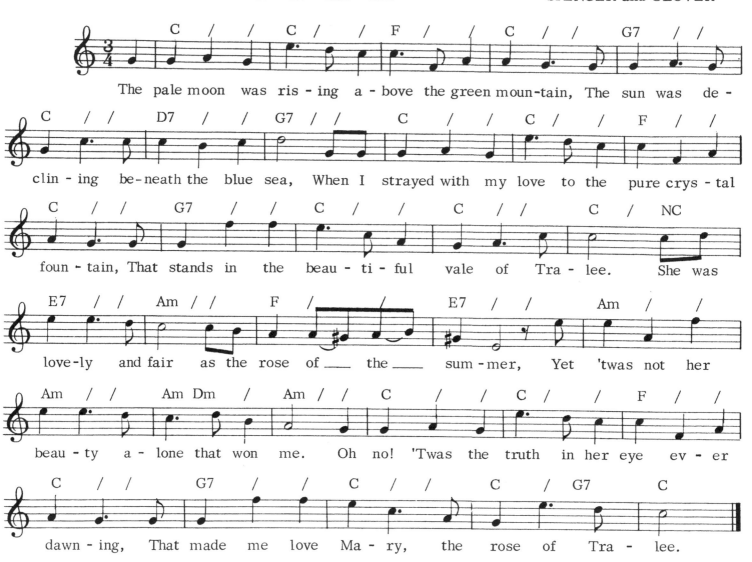

The pale moon was ris-ing a-bove the green moun-tain, The sun was de-clin-ing be-neath the blue sea, When I strayed with my love to the pure crys-tal foun-tain, That stands in the beau-ti-ful vale of Tra-lee. She was love-ly and fair as the rose of __ the __ sum-mer, Yet 'twas not her beau-ty a-lone that won me. Oh no! 'Twas the truth in her eye ev-er dawn-ing, That made me love Ma-ry, the rose of Tra-lee.

MY WILD IRISH ROSE

CHORDS: C - F - D7 - G7

CHAUNCEY OLCOTT

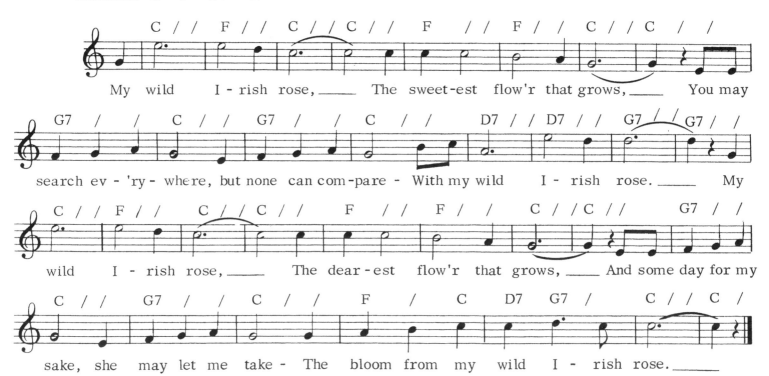

My wild I-rish rose, __ The sweet-est flow'r that grows, __ You may search ev-'ry-where, but none can com-pare - With my wild I-rish rose. __ My wild I-rish rose, __ The dear-est flow'r that grows, __ And some day for my sake, she may let me take - The bloom from my wild I-rish rose. __

BILL BAILEY

HUGHIE CANNON

I'VE BEEN WORKING ON THE RAILROAD

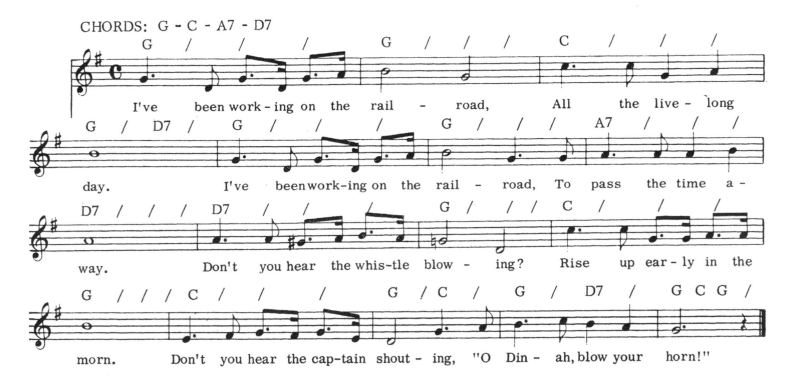

SANTA LUCIA

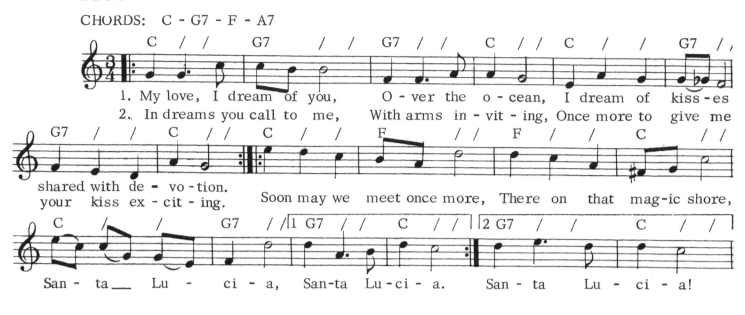

O SOLE MIO (My Sunshine)

EDUARDO DI CAPUA

GYPSY LOVE SONG

CHORDS: C - F - C7 - D7 - G7 - Am

SMITH and HERBERT

Slum - ber on, my lit - tle gyp - sy sweet-heart, Dream of the field and the grove. _____ Can you hear me, hear me in that dream-land, Where your fan - cies rove? _____ Slum - ber on, my lit - tle gyp - sy sweet - heart, Wild lit - tle wood - land dove. _____ Can you hear the song __ that __ tells you, All my _____ · heart's true love? _____

THE SWEETEST STORY EVER TOLD

CHORDS: F - Bb - Gm - Dm - C7 - D7 - G7

R. M. STULTS

Tell me, do you love me? Tell me soft - ly, sweet - ly, as of old!
Tell me that you love me, For that's the sweet-est sto - ry ev - er told.
Tell me, do you love me? Whis - per soft - ly, sweet-ly, as of old.
Tell me that you love me, For that's the sweet-est sto - ry ev - er told.

THE STAR SPANGLED BANNER

CHORDS: F - B♭ - C7 - D7 - G7 - Gm

Words by FRANCIS SCOTT KEY
Music by JOHN STAFFORD SMITH

THE BATTLE HYMN OF THE REPUBLIC

STEFFE & HOWE

CHORDS: C - G7 - F - Dm

2. I have seen Him in the watch-fires of a hundred circling camps,
They have build-ed Him an altar in the evening dews and damps.
I can read His righteous sentence by the dim and flaring lamps,
His day is marching on.   (Repeat Refrain)

3. He has sounded forth the trumpet that shall never call retreat,
He is sifting out the hearts of men before His judgment seat.
Oh, be swift, my soul, to answer Him! Be jubilant, my feet!
Our God is marching on.   (Repeat Refrain)

AMERICA

CHORDS: F - C7 - B♭ - Dm - Gm

SAMUEL F. SMITH (Text)

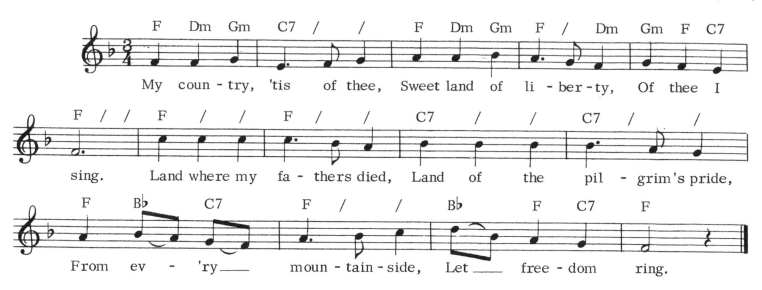

My coun - try, 'tis of thee, Sweet land of li - ber - ty, Of thee I
sing. Land where my fa - thers died, Land of the pil - grim's pride,
From ev - 'ry ___ moun - tain - side, Let ___ free - dom ring.

2. My native country, thee, land of the noble free,
Thy name I love.
I love thy rocks and rills, thy woods and templed hills,
My heart with rapture thrills like that above.

3. Let music swell the breeze, and ring from all the trees,
Sweet freedom's song.
Let mortal tongues awake, let all that breathe partake,
Let rocks their silence break, the sound prolong.

4. Our fathers' God, to Thee, author of liberty, To Thee we sing.
Long may our land be bright with freedom's holy light,
Protect us by Thy might, Great God, Our King!

AMERICA THE BEAUTIFUL

CHORDS: C - F - G7 - A7 - C7

WARD and BATES

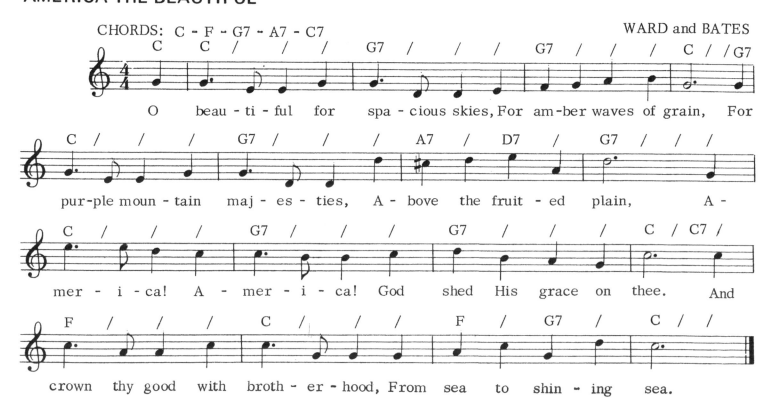

O beau - ti - ful for spa - cious skies, For am - ber waves of grain, For
pur - ple moun - tain maj - es - ties, A - bove the fruit - ed plain, A -
mer - i - ca! A - mer - i - ca! God shed His grace on thee. And
crown thy good with broth - er - hood, From sea to shin - ing sea.

HAIL TO THE CHIEF

Words: ALBERT GAMSE
Music: JAMES SANDERSON

CHORDS: C - F - G7

Hail to the Chief we have chos-en for the na-tion, Hail to the Chief! We sa-lute him, one and all. Hail to the Chief, as we pledge co-op-er-a-tion - In proud ful-fill-ment of a great, no-ble call. Yours is the aim to make this grand coun-try grand-er, This you will do, That's our strong, firm be-lief. Hail to the one we se-lect-ed as com-mand-er, Hail to the Pres-i-dent! Hail to the Chief!

WHEN JOHNNY COMES MARCHING HOME

CHORDS: Gm - Bb - D7

When John-ny comes marching home a-gain, Hur-rah! Hur-rah! We'll give him a heart-y wel-come then, Hur-rah! Hur-rah! Oh the men will cheer and the boys will shout, The la-dies they will all turn out, And we'll all feel gay, When John-ny comes march-ing home.

BEAUTIFUL ISLE OF SOMEWHERE

ABIDE WITH ME

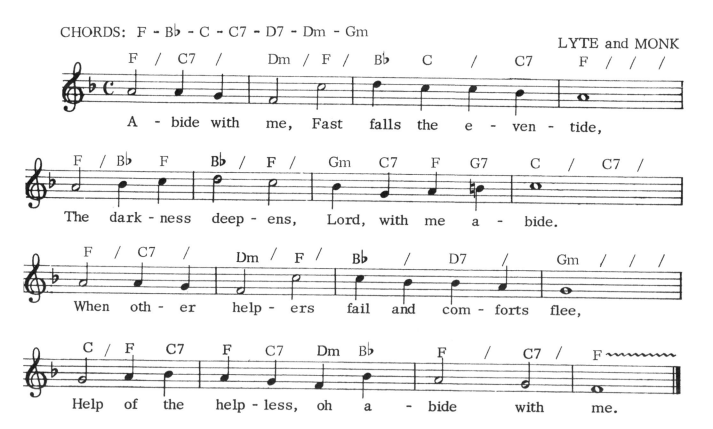

THE ROSARY

Words by ROBERT ROGERS
Music by ETHELBERT NEVIN

CHORDS: C - F - C7 - G7 - A7 - E7 - Am

Note the use of sweeping glissandos over all strings.

The hours I spent with thee, dear heart, _____ Are as a string of pearls to me. _____ I count them o - ver ev - 'ry one a - part, My ro - sa - ry, my ro - sa - ry! Each hour a pearl, each pearl a pray'r, _____ To still a heart in ab - sence wrung, _____ I tell each bead un - to the end, And there a cross is hung! Oh mem-o - ries that bless and burn! _____ Oh bar-ren gain and bit - ter loss! _____ I kiss each bead and strive at last to learn, To kiss the cross, sweet - heart! To kiss the cross. _____

WHISPERING HOPE

CHORDS: C - F - D7 - G7 - Am

ALICE HAWTHORNE

ONWARD, CHRISTIAN SOLDIERS

ARTHUR S. SULLIVAN
SABINE BARING - GOULD

CHORDS: C - F - G - D7 - G7

ROCK OF AGES

CHORDS: C - F - G7

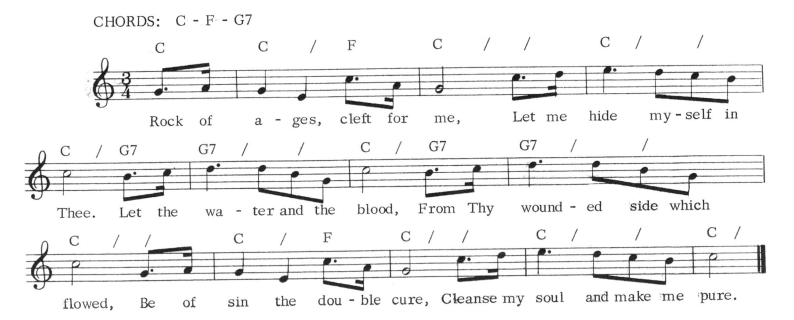

2. While I draw this fleeting breath, till my eyelids close in death,
   When I soar to worlds unknown, and behold Thee on Thy throne,
   Rock of ages, cleft for me, Let me hide myself in Thee!

STRUMMING AND PICKING MELODIES

The strums you have played on the Autoharp have served to accompany the voice. You will need to practise quite a bit, but it's rewarding to use your Autoharp as a solo instrument for playing your favorite melodies, with or without vocal rendition.

This is accomplished by melody STRUMMING or PICKING. In strumming, it is better to place the instrument on table or lap rather than holding it upright. The upright position is preferred in melody picking.

You may strum the strings to the left of the chords, but many melody strummers prefer to stroke the strings at the right of the bars, because they can clearly see the scale label which appears on most Autoharps.

The scale label is here shown. Small white numbers are printed under the strings in units of five, showing the specific area in which your right hand plays.

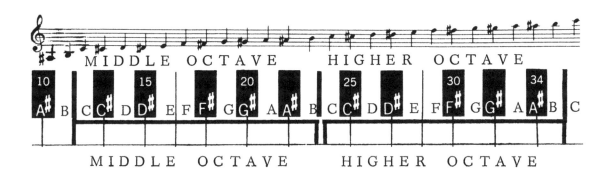

We use CHORD SYMBOLS just like before, but now you must stop your stroke at the string number corresponding to the note of the melody.

For example, G-20 means:

DEPRESS THE G CHORD, WHILE STROKING UP FROM THE BOTTOM TO NUMBER 20, LETTING THE STROKE END AT THIS NUMBER.

It's not as difficult as it sounds to reach the right string. When a button is depressed, the adjacent strings are silenced. So (on each side of the wanted note) you have a field of silence before the melody note sounds.

"Picking" a melody is more difficult. Finger picks are recommended because the "pick" will produce a louder sound. It involves a pinch of the thumb and index finger followed by the proper number of strums played by the thumb, depending of course on the structure of the tune. In "picking" a melody, the index finger hits only one string.

In strumming, you may stroke with the fleshy part of the thumb or the nail of the index finger, or with thumb pick. With practice, your ear will guide you surprisingly well to the right notes!

The table below will give you, by letters and music notes, each number used in the melodies which follow.   The encircled numbers are printed on your guide.   The table may also prove useful in assigning numbers to melodies not included in this book.

NOTE NUMBER	NAME OF NOTE	POSITION ON STAFF	
9	A		LOW SECTION
(10)	A♯ or B♭		
11	B		
12	C		MIDDLE SECTION
13	C♯ or D♭		
14	D		
(15)	E♭		
16	E		
17	F		
18	F♯ or G♭		
19	G		
(20)	G♯ or A♭		
21	A		
22	A♯ or B♭		
23	B		
24	C		HIGH SECTION
(25)	C♯ or D♭		
26	D		
27	E♭		
28	E		
29	F		
(30)	F♯ or G♭		
31	G		

Practise slowly with a few scales, stroking up to the numbered notes. A chord accompanies each note.

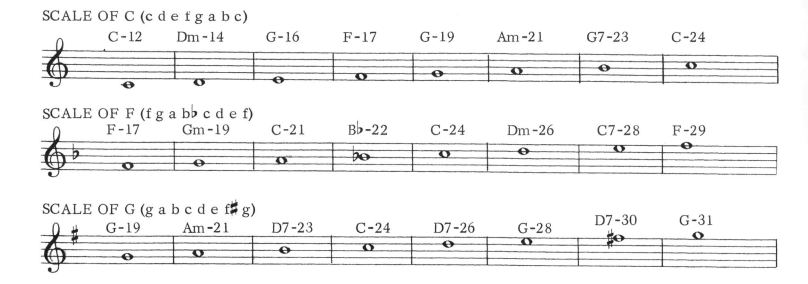

Now, press the C chord and stroke to the given numbers for "TAPS", playing every note with an upstroke of the right thumb:

TAPS

CHORD: C only   NUMBERS: 19-24-28-31

You are now ready to try some well known tunes, starting with the popular "Birthday Theme".

We suggest you study the following numbers, locating their position on the Autoharp, before attempting to play the piece:

12 - 14 - 16 - 17 - 19 - 21 - 22 - 24

BIRTHDAY THEME

CHORDS: C - F - B♭

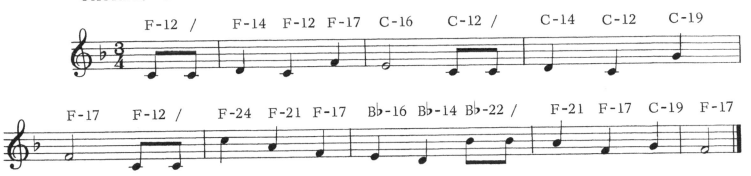

Please note, in connection with the selection which follows, measure No. 4 and similar measures, the CHORD should be held for the full time value but the stroke need not be repeated.

Where the same chord governs two or more differently numbered notes, hold the chord on the first number, while stroking to the ensuing numbers.

Incidentally, the strokes may but need not always start from the bottom string. You may start the stroke about 8 or 10 notes below the melody note and continue to the melody string.

DRINK TO ME ONLY WITH THINE EYES

CHORDS: C - F - Dm - G7 (solo or vocal)

86

NOBODY KNOWS THE TROUBLE I'VE SEEN

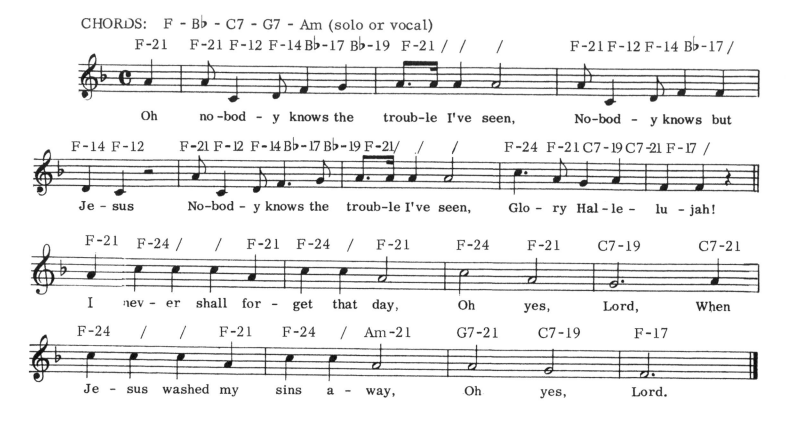

JACOB'S LADDER

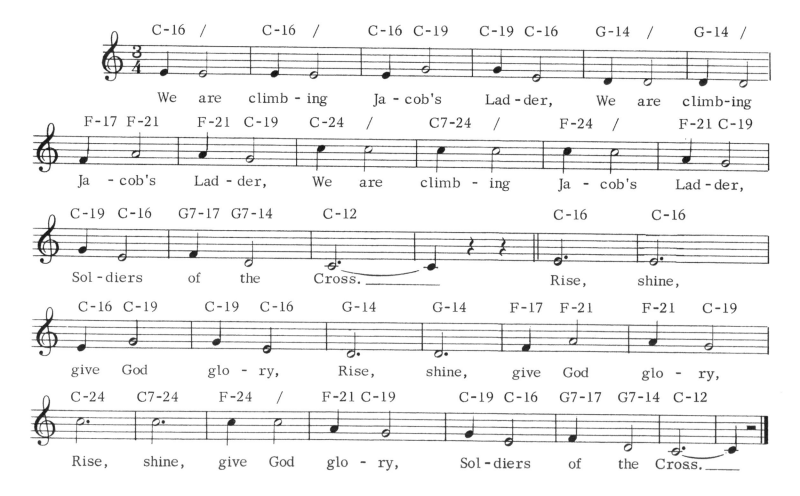

WHEN THE SAINTS GO MARCHING IN

CHORDS: C - G7 - F - G

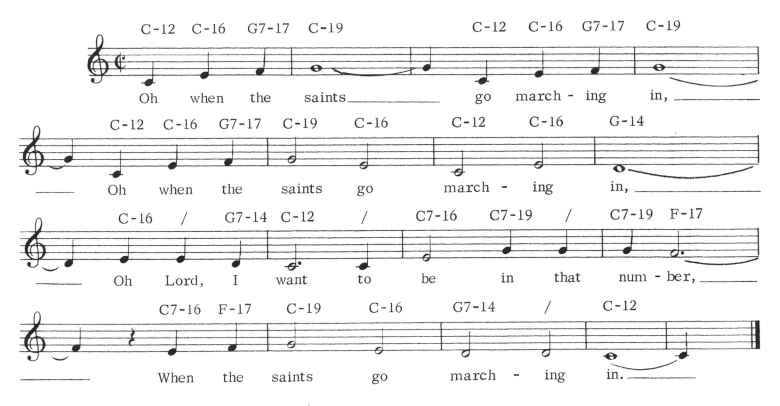

CARELESS LOVE

CHORDS: F - Bb - C7

ON THE SLOOP "JOHN B"

CHORDS: G - C - D7 - G7

THE OLD GRAY MARE

CHORDS: C7 - F - B♭

OLD MacDONALD

CHORDS: G - C - D7

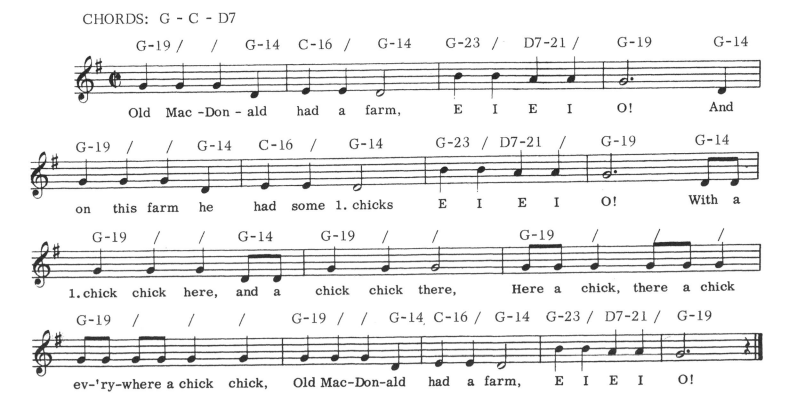

2. ducks (quack quack)   3. pigs (oink oink)   4. turkeys (gobble gobble)   5. cows (moo moo)

WILDWOOD FLOWER

CHORDS: C - C7 - F - G7

I'll en - twine and I'll min - gle my ra - ven black
Oh he prom - ised to love me, He called me his

hair, _____ With the ros - es so red and the li - lies so
flow'r, _____ Lit - tle flow'r of the wild - wood to cheer ev - 'ry

fair. _____ I a - woke from my dream and my i - dol was
hour. _____ And I'll pray night and day he'll re - gret this dark

clay, His wild - wood flow - er fad - ed, He threw it a - way. _____
hour, When he, my love, dis - card - ed His frail wild - wood flow'r. _____

THE WEEPING WILLOW TREE

CHORDS: G - G7 - C - D7

1. Bur - y me be - neath the

wil - low, 'Neath the weep - ing wil - low tree, _____

_____ When he comes and finds me

sleep - ing, Then per - haps he'll think of me. _____

BLOW THE MAN DOWN

CHORDS: F - C7 - D7 - Gm

THIS OLD MAN

CHORDS: F - B♭ - C7

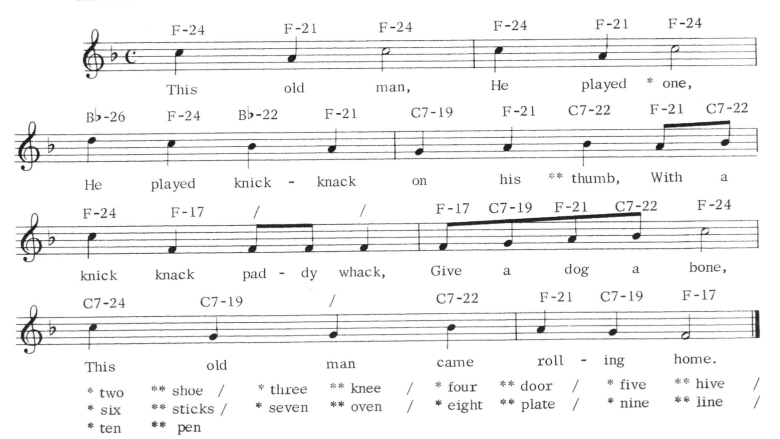

This old man, He played * one,
He played knick - knack on his ** thumb, With a
knick knack pad - dy whack, Give a dog a bone,
This old man came roll - ing home.

* two   ** shoe /   * three   ** knee /   * four   ** door /   * five   ** hive /
* six   ** sticks /   * seven   ** oven /   * eight   ** plate /   * nine   ** line /
* ten   ** pen

DIXIE

CHORDS: C - F - C7 - D7 - G7

DANIEL D. EMMETT

THE YELLOW ROSE OF TEXAS

CHORDS: C - F - G7 - Dm

MELODY OF LOVE

CHORDS: F - C - D7 - G - Gm

H. ENGELMANN

BLUE DANUBE WALTZ

CHORDS: C - F - G7

JOHANN STRAUSS

LULLABY

CHORDS: C - F - G7

JOHANNES BRAHMS

LARGO ("New World Symphony")

ANTON DVORAK

CHORDS: C - F - G - Am

HOME SWEET HOME

CHORDS: C - F - G - G7

Words by JOHN H. PAYNE
Music by HENRY R. BISHOP